The Future of Work

The Future of Work

How Artificial Intelligence Can Augment Human Capabilities

Yassi Moghaddam, Heather Yurko,
Haluk Demirkan, Nathan Tymann, and
Ammar Rayes

BEP BUSINESS EXPERT PRESS

The Future of Work: How Artificial Intelligence Can Augment Human Capabilities

Copyright © Business Expert Press, LLC, 2020.

Cover image licensed by Ingram Image, StockPhotoSecrets.com

Cover and interior design by Exeter Premedia Services Private Ltd., Chennai, India

First published in 2020 by
Business Expert Press, LLC
222 East 46th Street, New York, NY 10017
www.businessexpertpress.com

ISBN-13: 978-1-95152-718-1 (paperback)
ISBN-13: 978-1-95152-719-8 (e-book)

Business Expert Press Collaborative Intelligence Collection

Collection ISSN: 2691-1779 (print)
Collection ISSN: 2691-1795 (electronic)

First edition: 2020

10 9 8 7 6 5 4 3 2 1

Printed in the United States of America.

Abstract

Jobs, and nature of work as we know it, are changing rapidly. As companies become more "digital," employees need to be empowered to become more innovative. Disruptive changes to work behaviors and business models will have a profound impact on the nature of work and worker. In many industries and countries, the most in-demand occupations, specialties, and skills did not exist ten or even five years ago, and the pace of change is set to accelerate. This will have a tremendous impact on how the workforce of the future acquires and applies new skills, and how companies organize work to stay nimble and competitive.

In this book, experts from industry and academia explore these trends and discuss how innovative companies are leveraging Artificial Intelligence and intelligent tools to make the workforce more inclusive, and enhance and augment human worker rather than replace it.

Keywords

skills; future of work; artificial intelligence; intelligence augmentation; AI; IA; cognitive computing; future of jobs; policy; reskilling; upskilling

Contents

Preface

Since 2015, the International Society of Service Innovation Professionals (ISSIP, see http://issi.org) has been running Discovery Summits[1] bringing together speakers and participants with an interest in better understanding intersection of a leading-edge technology trends and total user experience and explore how institutions and individuals can leverage the value cocreation opportunities that exist at these intersections for the benefit of business and society. Over the last couple of years, we have been exploring how the nature of work and jobs are changing in the face of rapid technological changes. We have been exploring topics including job vs. task automation, liquid workforce, skills needed for current/future roles, impact of Artificial intelligence (AI) to the workplace and workforce, how can AI be used to help reskill workers that are impacted by AI, the role of technological advances such as bots, AI, intelligent assistants, Internet of Things (IoT), and policy implication of the changing world of work.

This book is based on a call for chapters that was sent out to participants at an ISSIP Discovery Summit held on September 27, 2018.

To create this book, we invited academic scholars and industry professionals with expertise in all areas of future of work who spoke or participated in that summit to write a short paper/chapter. Industry, academic, and policy perspectives are presented here.

As digitization, fueled by advancement in machine learning and data science, is disrupting markets and industries, institutions as corporations, educational establishments, and governments are grappling to take advantage of the tremendous opportunities and address significant challenges caused by these seismic shifts. These shifts have implications at the organization, team, and individual levels. Innovative organization are redesigning work and providing workforce retraining opportunities to ensure machines are enhancing, not replacing, human capabilities as they

---

[1] More details about ISSIP Discovery Summits: http://issip.org/issip-discovery-summit/

are transforming for exponential growth in the digital economy. Innovative teams are adapting agile practices to be more dynamic and respond to the fast-changing market forces by leveraging the best of people and technology. Innovative individuals are welcoming life-long learning to acquire the skills that enables them to upskill and stay in demand.

The ISSIP BEP Future of Work collection explores these topics and aims to offer insights and practical wisdom easily applicable to the workplace.

Potential beneficiaries of these books include executives and middle managers, professionals and practitioners who are seeking either to acquire new skills or refresh and update their knowledge of existing ones, and advanced business, MBA, and EMBA students.

Questions that we continue to seek better and better answers include:

- How is organization of work changing? What are the drivers and enablers?
- What is the role of lifelong learning in future of work and learning?
- How is the definition of enterprise changing?
- What is the evolution of roles and skills?
- What is the impact of Intelligent Assistants in future of work?
- How is IoT impacting future of work
- How is robotics impacting future of work?
- How can we design ethical AI?
- What are the implication of dynamic sourcing of talent to individuals, institutions, and society?
- What is the role leadership and management in future of work?
- How should policies change?
- How will work evolve in the future?
- How can IT, HR, product groups, and marketing be the driver of innovation for digital transformation and future of work?

We hope readers find this book a thought-provoking springboard for advancing their understanding of how work is changing today and how they can better prepare for the opportunities and challenges in this fast-changing landscape of work.

Yassi Moghaddam, Santa Clara, CA
Heather Yurko, New York, NY
Haluk Demirkan, Tacoma, WA
Nathan Tymann, Durham, NC
Ammar Rayes, San Jose, CA
March 21, 2019

Acknowledgments

The five coeditors wish to thank all the chapter authors, P. K. Agrawal, Terri Griffith, Stephen Kwan, Jim Spohrer, and Pankaj Srivastava, for their contributions to this book. In addition to the chapter authors, we would like to thank other speakers including Martin Fleming, Alex Kass, Ashwin Ram, Preetha Ram, and Ann Majchrz. Furthermore, we want to thank Dan Moshavi, Dean, Lucas College and Graduate School of Business, San Jose State University (SJSU), for his continued support of ISSIP including graciously hosting the ISSIP Discovery Summit. Finally, we would like to thank all the Summit participants (see Appendix) some of whom responded to the call for chapters and all of whom contributed to the thought-provoking discussions that culminated in this book.

CHAPTER 1

Introduction: Preparing for the Jobs of Tomorrow Today

Yassi Moghaddam

Advances in artificial intelligence (AI) fueled by machine learning are disrupting the way we live and work. AI will have wide-ranging impact on institutions, employment, jobs, wages, and income distribution, as machines emulate or exceed human capabilities. This phenomenon will create tremendous opportunities for economic progress, societal advancement, and individual prosperity and growth. Realizing these growing opportunities for a thriving future, however, will depend on significant collaboration today between different stakeholders from all sectors of society including industry, academia, government, and entrepreneurs.

The International Society of Service Innovation Professionals (ISSIP, see http://issip.org) is a nonprofit professional association established in 2012 to bring diverse stakeholders to study the impact of digitization on business, individuals, and society to help institutions and the individual navigate the complexities and exciting opportunities of value cocreation in our global digital economy. In ISSIP, communities of practice involving practitioners, students, faculty, policy makers, and others interested in advancing innovation in business and society come together to study and improve service ecosystems. Work, as a rapidly changing service ecosystem, fueled by disruptive technologies including AI and data analytics, is of particular interest to the ISSIP community. That is why since 2017 we have held a number of Discovery Summits, and workshops on this topic to help our members better prepare today for the opportunities and challenges of future of work.

The chapters of this book are written by attendees of the Future of Work Discovery Summits held in 2017 and 2018, both held at San Jose State University Lucas College and Graduate School of Business. In 2017, we explored how work environments are changing and in 2018 we explored how jobs are changing.

Most of the chapters in this book, chapters 2 to 5, are written by industry leaders who are either involved in AI and future of work research or are involved in the implementation of change in their enterprise that prepares the workforce today to be ready for the challenges and opportunities of tomorrow's workplace. Chapters 6 to 9 were written by thought leaders from academia with perspectives on how individual lifelong learning and policy implications.

Chapter 2 by Tymann provides a perspective on the importance of individuals to lifelong learning and the roles of institutions to support lifelong learning of their workforce. Chapter 3 by Rayes outlines a map for what machine learning skills will continue to be in demand in decades to come. Chapter 4 by Srivastava provides a glimpse as to how AI is being leveraged to reskill the workforce. Chapter 5 by Spohrer offers a perspective on the importance of entrepreneurship in the future of work. Chapter 6 by Griffith proposes four dimensions that we all need to manage to be success in work and life. Chapter 7 by Agrawal lays out policy challenges and opportunities. And finally, Chapter 8 by Kwan provides recent views of U.S. government regarding the future of jobs and AI.

Looking at common themes across the chapters, it becomes apparent that tasks that are most prone to automation involve activities in highly structured and predictable environments. Generally, tasks will be automated, not jobs. It is important for all workers whether they are in tech or other industries to be digitally savvy and be AI literate. Some jobs, however, will be displaced. So, reskilling and lifelong learning is an imperative for every professional. Policy makers must deploy policies that encourage reskilling in high-risk sectors to support a digital economy in which institutions and individuals thrive.

PART I
Industry Perspective

CHAPTER 2

How Organizations Should Prepare for AI

Nathan Tymann

Abstract

In today's workplace, it is critically important that people and organizations be adaptable. Increased market pressures, competition, and the rapid pace of change brought about by technology require a nimbleness that wasn't needed in the past. Specifically, artificial intelligence and machine learning are likely to influence the future of work in ways that require new ways of thinking about job roles. This chapter begins by discussing how the future of work is being scripted due to the influence of artificial intelligence and machine learning. Next is an overview of research on the importance of continuous learning for individuals, teams, and organizations, followed by an examination of the type of leadership that learning organizations require to foster a culture of innovation, creativity, and stability. To close, a discussion of what these changing times mean for measuring job performance and for hiring the right people has been added.

One exciting part about working today is that technology gives us the opportunity to figure out what makes us uniquely human within the context of work. Technologies such as artificial intelligence and machine learning are making it possible to continue to offload certain critical, but transactional, job functions to free us up to perform job roles that humans do best. According to a recent article by the World Economic Forum (2018), this dynamic driven by technology is accelerating the evolution of the future of work into three types of jobs.

Figure 2.1 New types of jobs

Image credits: Center for generational kinetics

The first type includes jobs that some people are afraid about losing, but really shouldn't be. These are predictable or highly repetitive jobs that don't require intuition or judgment. These include jobs that computer programs perform better than humans. We've seen this dynamic since the Industrial Revolution and in manufacturing plants for a long time. These include many data entry jobs or other administrative jobs. Self-driving trucks are being experimented to replace human drivers on routes that travel through remotely populated areas. By enabling jobs like those to go to machines, humans are free to aspire to the next two categories of jobs.

The second category includes collaborating with the machine. Think of the evolution of these types of jobs as akin to what the advent of better tools meant to skilled craftsman over the centuries. A civil engineer used to rely on measurements and calculations done by hand to build a bridge, but now she will use computers and software to enable her to perform her task with more elegance and efficiency. Surgeons can now use computer-guided lasers to excise tumors with greater precision than most could accomplish with their hands.

The third category of jobs includes those that cannot be performed by machines. Jobs in the creative arts are in this category, along with other roles that require design, judgment, leadership, entrepreneurship, or innovation.

The benefits that technology provides are here to stay. So how do organizations adjust to maximize the creative and innovative capabilities that only humans offer while sustaining organizational excellence?

Organizational leaders need to foster a culture of continuous learning where new ideas and concepts are discussed and used to create innovation. Research shows that organizations cannot create innovative ideas by themselves, but they can create conditions by which teams can learn. Then teams can distribute new knowledge for the benefit of the entire organization (Stelmaszczyk 2016).

The Need to Embrace Continuous Learning

Team learning and organizational learning are different, but they are closely related. Team learning requires that teachers and learners actively collaborate to leverage the strengths of the teachers and that learning can be absorbed by the learners (Goolsarran, Hamo, Lane, Frawley, and Lu 2018). Within most teams, however, the teacher role and learner roles rotate because individuals on the team are experts in different bodies of knowledge. Team learning is a connector between learning at the individual level and learning at the organizational level. Research shows a linear relationship between individual learning, team learning, and organizational learning. According to Stelmaszczyk (2016), individual learning is manifested within teams. Team learning occurs when individuals communicate, test, and implement knowledge that they bring into the team. The collective knowledge of many teams represents organizational learning. While organizations benefit by the implementation of knowledge by teams, they cannot create knowledge on their own (Stelmaszczyk 2016).

Crossan, Lane, and White (1999) described organizational learning using the 4I model: intuiting, interpreting, integrating, and institutionalizing. The 4I framework posits that there are subconnections within an organization that span across individuals, teams, and organizations (Schilling, and Kluge 2009). Intuiting refers to the way in which individuals gain new ideas based on their own personal experiences. Interpreting happens when an individual explains what he knows to other people, either through words or actions. Integrating occurs at the team

- Intuiting (individuals)
- Interpreting (individuals)
- Integrating (teams)
- Institutionalizing (organizations)

Figure 2.2 4I's for organizational learning

level when knowledge is shared more widely until it becomes common understanding within a team and then the team uses the knowledge to act. Finally, institutionalizing is when shared knowledge forms the organizational infrastructure through applied systems, processes, policies, and strategies. Therefore, organizational learning includes all four of these phases, inclusive of and dependent upon, individual learning and team learning (Schilling, and Kluge 2009).

One example of an implementation of the relationship between team learning and organizational learning took place at a cancer treatment center in the United States (Valentine 2018). In this study, project leads, managers, and clinical operations staff members from across the cancer treatment center provided individual input through their functional teams to benefit the entire organization. A challenge in the study was the attempt to synchronize inputs from one team to another. Leaders needed to work with their teams to institutionalize their combined knowledge, creating rules and systems for the entire organization to use. However, one of the conclusions of the study was that collaboration took great effort and time on the part of all members of the organization even though their knowledge sharing was conducted with friendliness and positive intentions. There was so much complexity involved in gathering requirements and sharing knowledge from one person to another, that integrating learning within a small team structure was the only way that the organization would be able to eventually institutionalize learning (Valentine 2018). This study demonstrated that team learning was the key connector between individual learning and organizational learning.

Overcoming Obstacles to Becoming
a Learning Organization

There are many obstacles to overcome when transforming an organization to a learning organization. According to McKenna (2017), four obstacles to change include a fear of failure, fear of the loss of competence, lack of trust, and a lack of commitment to change. Fear of failure causes paralysis for people who are afraid to take a risk. This fear can prevent an organization from giving the proposed change a chance to be adopted before giving up. Fear of the loss of competence especially affects experts in a given job role who think that transformational changes may make their special abilities irrelevant. Lack of trust can go in any direction of the organizational hierarchy. Often people do not trust the leaders in their organizations to make the right decisions or to lead them in the right direction. Also, sometimes leaders do not trust that their people are skilled enough or adaptable enough to accomplish a new goal regardless of the quality of their own leadership. Finally, lack of commitment to change occurs when leadership changes their focus so often that people see the next change initiative as just the flavor of the month. All these obstacles are poisonous when leaders attempt to create a learning organization because they are so self-centered and negative.

Systems thinking increases the number of available options for overcoming fear of failure, fear of the loss of competence, lack of trust, and lack of commitment to change. Two important characteristics of general systems theory are seeing an organization as an open system and emphasizing the interrelationship of smaller wholes bounded within a larger collective whole (von Bertalanffy 1968). Viewing an organization as an open system should drive leaders to hold loosely to narrow organizational identities, because an open system implies that the organization needs new ideas from the teams and individuals within it. The vulnerability that leaders show by embracing the concept of an open system brings down barriers between leaders and followers. According to Vaughn (2016), leaders should admit to their people that they do not always know what the best decision is, and that if they fail, then they will fail together. Similarly, while the competence of people who perform well today may not be the same skills they need to succeed tomorrow, the organization will support people with training to enable them to learn new competencies. By providing people with support and training that they need to succeed and by emphasizing the interrelationship of smaller wholes within a larger whole, people within teams see the importance their contributions make to the overall organization. As a result, leaders build trust between themselves and their teams.

Lack of commitment to change requires another strategy for overcoming obstacles to change into a learning organization. According to McKenna (2017), there are five good options by which team learning can influence the change process. The first option is to learn from outside experts to gain perspective on how one organization compares with another. The second is to invest in a pilot project to implement barrier-breaking actions on a small scale before deciding whether to expand the actions across the entire organization. The third is to appeal to people's natural sense of rewards for work done well by beginning a routine that celebrates good behaviors. The fourth is to pull in internal people to volunteer to work together on small teams and then present their findings to leadership. The fifth is to issue a survey to the organization asking for honest, anonymous feedback. It is best for leaders to try one or several of these approaches to increase the likelihood that they are going to be successful in creating a learning organization.

In summary, a healthy organization is one that delivers value to its stakeholders for a sustained amount of time. However, an organization needs to adjust to changing markets and competitive pressures to be sustainable. This sustainability can only be achieved when an organization becomes a learning organization with an influx of innovative ideas (Cai, and Li 2018). Leaders will face obstacles in becoming a learning organization, so they need to use strategies to foster a culture of continuous learning where new ideas and concepts are discussed and used to create innovation (Vaughn 2016). When leaders are successful in creating a learning organization, then the entire organization will benefit (Stelmaszczyk 2016).

Importance of Collaborative Leadership

Organizations will not be sustainable over time unless they adapt to changing market conditions and evolve to overcome competitive pressures. Therefore, leaders need to infuse a culture of innovation and creativity into their organizations to remain adaptable (Boylan, and Turner 2017). Collaborative leadership is an effective method to enable the growth of innovation and creativity, which results in maintaining a sustainable organization (Steiner 2009).

A collaborative leader plays an important role in creating a culture and attitude that enables an organization to meet the objectives of today and will also prepare the organization to overcome the challenges of tomorrow (Boylan, and Turner 2017). A collaborative leader brings stakeholders together to engage in decision making through sharing of knowledge and experiences (Ansell, and Gash 2008). He recognizes that he needs the expertise of other people to solve complex problems, because he doesn't have all the best answers (Levine 2011). There are many advantages to using a collaborative leadership approach. For example, a collaborative leader introduces a diversity of perspectives to the organization by connecting key resources together across any functional boundaries that may exist. This diversity of perspectives brings a fresh and unbiased view to the organization, which fosters a culture of continuous learning (Cuellar, Krist, Nichols, and Kuzel 2018). Also, a collaborative leader empowers her team to recommend decisions as a team, after ideas are shared and expected outcomes are understood. This feeling of empowerment encourages members of the organization to identify with the organization and to care about the success that the organization can achieve (Boylan, and Turner 2017).

One potential disadvantage to a collaborative leadership approach includes the threat of collaboration overload (Cross, Rebele, and Grant 2016). Effective collaboration requires participants to sustain energy and effort. If too much demand is placed on certain individuals, then they may experience burnout. Another potential disadvantage is that collaboration can result in decisions being delayed while different perspectives are being considered. An extreme case of delaying decisions is commonly called "analysis paralysis," where people become so weighed down with considering every possible decision that all forward progress stops (Bensoussan and Fleisher 2013).

Benefits of Collaboration for Innovation and Creativity

A learning organization has a culture that encourages people to collaborate both within their own teams and also with stakeholders outside their teams (Crossan et al. 1999; Steiner 2009). The leaders of learning organizations set the expectation that everyone needs to continually learn and share knowledge with the others in the organization. Jain (2015) supports the same conclusion by writing that collaboration enhances innovative behaviors. Since collaboration is present within a learning organization, a learning organization supports innovative behaviors as well. In addition, when effective collaboration takes place in an organization, people will strive to contribute innovative behaviors even if those behaviors are beyond what is expected of them within their normal job roles (Panaccio, Henderson, Liden, Wayne, and Cao 2015).

Relationship of Innovation and Creativity With Sustainability

An effective leader will test and then implement innovative ideas that improve the organization by making it more efficient, effective, and adaptable to changing needs. The implementation of good, new ideas provides sustainability to an organization. For example, nonprofit organizations face many pressures that threaten their sustainability, including limited financial resources. Nonprofits need to attract financial supporters as well as dedicated people who choose to remain affiliated with the crowded group of organizations that compete for their participation (Wemmer, Emrich, & Koenigstorfer 2016). Wemmer et al. (2016) conducted a quantitative study of 292 nonprofit board members in Germany, examining the effectiveness of collaboration to maintain stable organizations within nonprofit sports clubs. The researchers concluded that sports clubs who collaborated with competing sports clubs had greater instances of innovation. Innovation enabled by sharing operational best practices led to the creation of new services and operational processes that enabled the sport clubs to become more efficient, more competitive, and more sustainable.

Another example of innovation and creativity encouraging sustainability was a qualitative case study that examined how women in Mexico used social innovation to achieve greater empowerment in a traditionally male-dominated society (Maguirre, Ruelas, and De La Torre 2016). After analyzing the data gathered in 70 interviews, Maguirre et al. (2016) concluded that the creation of gender-equality policies gave the women the opportunity to earn a living along with men. More importantly, these innovative policies empowered women to create their own businesses and to shift the focus on equality within the Mexican culture. As a result, this paved the way for both Mexican businesses and Mexican women in general to experience a more optimistic future outlook.

Balancing Innovation, Creativity, and Stability

It is a difficult, but critical, responsibility of organizational leaders that they balance the pursuits of innovation, creativity, and stability. According to Boylan and Turner (2017), there are four ways that leaders can achieve a proper balance of these factors. First is by communicating that the organization needs to take prudent risks. Taking prudent risks implies that leaders have a strategy that they believe will lead to stability and success, but they acknowledge that mistakes will likely occur along the journey. People don't need to fear that every mistake will result in catastrophic consequences. When leaders set expectations in this way, they establish an environment of psychological safety with their people.

Second, feeling psychologically safe will encourage people to generate and share new ideas. New ideas are essential ingredients for innovation and creativity. However, leaders need to discern whether an idea is likely to be useful in the short term or the long term, since not all new ideas will be beneficial for organizational success. Given this inherent uncertainty, the best approach that a leader can take is to encourage new ideas to continually flow in from his stakeholders as matter of normal practice (Boylan, and Turner 2017).

Third, a leader needs to facilitate collaboration inside and outside of her organization (Boylan, and Turner 2017; Steiner 2009). An important condition for a healthy collaboration is to include an allowance of dissenting opinions. A collaborative leader will ensure that people with diverse viewpoints are interacting, because the tension that is created by different ideas is necessary for adaptability, creativity, and learning that lead to organizational stability (Uhl-Bien, Marion, & McKelvey, 2007). Collaboration brings the opportunity to identify risks and then to strategize how to adapt to mitigate those risks.

Fourth, a leader needs to balance innovation, creativity, and stability by recognizing and rewarding good ideas that emerge from his organization

(Boylan and Turner 2017). Rewards can take many forms including financial prizes, public recognition, and commitment of resources to further develop the ideas into actions. The most important lesson that leaders can take about giving rewards is that it creates a cycle of continuous innovation within the organization when people are motivated to share their ideas and personally identify with the success of the organization.

In summary, organizations need to adapt to changing market conditions and evolve to overcome competitive pressures to be sustainable. Therefore, leaders need to infuse a culture of innovation and creativity into their organizations. An environment of psychological safety is an important prerequisite that leaders need to foster for collaboration to flourish (Boylan, and Turner 2017). Collaborative leadership is an effective way to enable innovation and creativity to grow, which results in a sustainable organization (Steiner 2009).

Measurement of Job Performance

It is important that employers use fair and effective hiring practices to build effective and sustainable organizations. Since employers rarely have complete knowledge of the traits that a job candidate possesses, they need to find ways to assess whether the candidate will be a good fit for any open job role using incomplete knowledge. Research on job performance supports that assumptions can be made between certain individual characteristics and future job performance (Van Iddekinge, and Ployhart 2008). Hiring managers can make better decisions by being aware of the conclusions that can be drawn from prior research.

Job performance can be measured according to several different dimensions. Four common measurements include task performance, citizenship performance, counterproductive work behavior, and adaptive performance (Van Iddekinge, and Ployhart 2008). First, task performance is the degree to which the results of an individual's work meets the required expectations for that job role (Tams, Thatcher, and Grover 2018). The specific measurements of task performance will vary from one job role to another, but they can often be categorized according to metrics that apply to financial, time-bound, customer service, or organizational development goals (Dhamayantie 2018). Next, citizenship performance, or organizational citizenship behavior, refers to interpersonal actions that create a positive work environment while supporting the overall business objectives of the organization (Becton, Carr, Mossholder, and Walker 2017). Citizenship performance is associated with the attitude that an individual displays at work. For example, someone who volunteers to help colleagues or who takes on extra work that is not within the scope of her own job responsibilities displays high citizenship performance (Van Iddekinge, and Ployhart 2008). Yet someone with high citizenship performance might also engage in counterproductive work behavior. According to Van Iddekinge and Ployhart (2008), counterproductive work behavior refers to actions that an individual takes that violates social norms or otherwise does not support a positive work environment. For example, Rehman and Shahnawaz (2018) researched the negative organizational impacts of theft, rumor spreading, and intentional absenteeism across several types of firms in India. Finally, adaptive performance is the ability for an individual to adjust his work behaviors to meet changing job or organizational expectations (Van Iddekinge, and Ployhart 2008). A good example of adaptive performance is the ability of successful salespeople to change the approaches that they use to sell products or services to customers with a wide range of business needs, budgets, and personalities (Wang, Wang, and Hou 2016).

Measurement of Predictors

While there are several lenses that can be used to measure job performance, there are two main categories that researchers use to describe predictors of individual job performance: cognitive ability and noncognitive ability. According to Woodley of Menie, Piffer, Peñaherrera, and Rindermann (2016), cognitive ability refers to a person's intelligence, with the term "g" referring to the general baseline of intelligence that most people inherently possess. The noncognitive predictor often studied is personality, which can be defined as the traits that a person most consistently displays in response to certain situations. One common approach to understanding personality is to examine the following five factors: conscientiousness, or the level of responsibility one feels to meet expectations; neuroticism, or emotional stability; extroversion, or the propensity that one has to work with others; agreeableness, or the desire to prioritize social relationships; and openness, or willingness to share with others (Judge, and Zapata, 2015). Researchers continue to study different combinations of these predictors to understand how they relate to building sustainable organizations (Wallace et al. 2016).

Predicting Job Performance

According to Wallace et al. (2016), it is understood that studying cognitive ability and personality traits in isolation cannot give complete insight into predicting organizational performance. Instead, studying the relationships between cognitive ability and personality traits within certain situations will yield the most valuable insights. One quantitative correlational study by Diedrich, Neubauer, and Ortner (2018) examined the role of both cognitive and noncognitive abilities to predict the job performance of 648 apprentices within diverse vocational areas in Austria. The authors concluded that there was a linear relationship between cognitive ability and job performance. However, the strongest predictor of job performance resulted from using an interactional approach where an intelligence measurement was combined with one of the five personality traits, namely conscientiousness. An important third variable used in this study was job satisfaction. In summary, the best job performance in this study was exhibited by participants with a combination of intelligence, satisfaction with their vocational area, and an inner drive to meet expectations.

Conclusions by Judge and Zapata (2015) supported the importance of the interactional approach as well. The authors conducted a quantitative correlational study to explore the degree to which each of the five personality traits was related to job performance in the literature. While they did not include measures of cognitive ability in their study, the authors did determine that there was a generally linear relationship between positive manifestations of each personality trait and job performance. However, Judge and Zapata (2015) concluded that the presence of certain personality traits within specific contexts were stronger indicators of job performance. For example, extroversion was a strong predictor of high performance in job roles that required social interaction and openness was a strong predictor of high performance in job roles that required creativity and innovation.

Improving the Hiring Process

Research on the relationships between cognitive ability and personality traits as predictors of job performance support three conclusions that can enable employers to make better hiring decisions. First, employers should understand that an interactional approach that combines measurements of cognitive ability and personality traits is effective because people cannot be characterized solely by their intelligence quotient (IQ) nor by a single personality trait. An interactional approach recognizes that there is an inherent complexity within individuals and that situational contexts will produce a wide range of possible performance outcomes (Dalal et al. 2015; Wallace et al. 2016). Second, while an employer should measure cognitive ability and personality traits, he should also determine the level of vocational interest that a job candidate has for the open position (Diedrich et al. 2018). This determination can be made through using open-ended questions in the interview process that ask the candidate to share their reasons for being interested in the job role for which they are applying (Weller et al. 2018). Third, an employer should understand the types of personality strengths that typically succeed in each job role, given the daily tasks and types of interactions that the jobs require (Judge, and Zapata 2015). This level of understanding can be gained by including subject matter experts in the interview panel and by providing opportunities for the most skilled employees to share the approaches that make them successful (Henry, McCarthy, Nannicelli, Seivert, and Vozenilek 2016).

It is important that employers hire the best people to build effective and sustainable organizations. Employers need to determine whether a candidate will be a good fit for any open job role using incomplete knowledge. Research that relates cognitive ability and personality traits with job performance can provide useful insights to predict future job performance to achieve organizational effectiveness (Dalal et al. 2015; Diedrich et al. 2018; Judge, and Zapata 2015; Van Iddekinge, and Ployhart 2008).

Conclusion

In some ways, the challenges that organizations and people face today are the same as those challenges that were faced in previous generations. However, artificial intelligence and machine learning are more than just the latest cycle of the working revolution. Global access to these technologies offer opportunities that are unprecedented. People and organizations who embrace these opportunities and build an infrastructure of continuous learning will lead their markets and help to define what the future of work will become.

Future jobs do require continuous learning with employees as both teachers and learners. Teacher and learner roles should be rotated because individuals on the team are experts in different bodies of knowledge and managers must create an adaptable culture of innovation and collaboration where employees are encouraged to work together and take risks.

References

Ansell, C., and A. Gash. 2008. "Collaborative Governance in Theory and Practice." *Journal of Public Administration Research & Theory* 18, no. 4, 543–571. Retrieved from https://lopes.idm.oclc.org/login?url=http://search. ebscohost.com/login.aspx?direct=true&db=bth&AN=34725965&site=eho st-live&scope=site

Becton, J.B., J.C. Carr, K.W. Mossholder, and H.J. Walker. 2017. "Differential Effects of Task Performance, Organizational Citizenship Behavior, and Job Complexity on Voluntary Turnover." *Journal of Business and Psychology* 32, no. 4, 495. doi: 10.1007/s10869-016-9461-x

Bensoussan, B.E., and C.S. Fleisher. 2013. *Analysis Without Paralysis : 12 Tools to Make Better Strategic Decisions.* Upper Saddle River, NJ: Pearson FT Press. Retrieved from https://lopes.idm.oclc.org/login?url=http: //search.ebscohost.com/login.aspx?direct=true&db=edsebk&AN=1598049 &site=eds-live&scope=site

Boylan, S.A., and K.A. Turner. 2017. "Developing Organizational Adaptability for Complex Environment." *Journal of Leadership Education* 16, no. 2, 183–198. Retrieved from https://lopes.idm.oclc.org/login?url=http: //search.ebscohost.com/login.aspx?direct=true&db=eric&AN=EJ1138760& site=eds-live&scope=sitehttp://www.journalofleadershiped.org/attachments/ article/503/0631_boylan.pdf

Cross, R., R. Rebele, and A. Grant. 2016. "Collaborative Overload: Too Much Teamwork Exhausts Employees and Saps Productivity. Here's How to Avoid it." *Harvard Business Review* 94, nos. (1–2), 74. Retrieved from https://lopes.idm.oclc.org/login?url=http://search.ebscohost.com/login.aspx?direct=true&db=edsggo&AN=edsgcl.438632758&site=eds-live&scope=site

Crossan, M.M., H.W. Lane, and R.E. White. 1999. "An Organizational Learning Framework: From Intuition to Institution." *The Academy of Management Review* 24, no. 3, 522. Retrieved from https://lopes.idm.oclc.org/login?url=http://search.ebscohost.com/login.aspx?direct=true&db=edsjsr&AN=edsjsr.259140&site=eds-live&scope=site

Cuellar, A., A.H. Krist, L.M. Nichols, and A.J. Kuzel. 2018. "Effect of Practice Ownership on Work Environment, Learning Culture, Psychological Safety, and Burnout." *The Annals of Family Medicine* 16, no. (Suppl 1), pp. S44–S51.

Dalal, R.S., R.D. Meyer, R.P. Bradshaw, J.P. Green, E.D. Kelly, and M. Zhu. 2015. "Personality Strength and Situational Influences on Behavior: A Conceptual Review and Research Agenda." *Journal of Management* 41, no. 1, 261–287. doi: 10.1177/0149206314557524

Dhamayantie, E. 2018. "Designing a Balanced Scorecard for Cooperatives." *International Journal of Organizational Innovation* 11, no. 2, 220–227. Retrieved from https://lopes.idm.oclc.org/login?url=http://search.ebscohost.com/login.aspx?direct=true&db=bth&AN=132233508&site=eds-live&scope=site

Diedrich, J., A.C. Neubauer, and A. Ortner. 2018. "The Prediction of Professional Success in Apprenticeship: The Role of Cognitive and Non-cognitive Abilities, of Interests and Personality." *International Journal for Research in Vocational Education and Training* 5, no. 2, 82–111. doi: 10.13152/IJRVET.5.2.1

Goolsarran, N., C.E. Hamo, S. Lane, S. Frawley, and W.H. Lu. 2018. "Effectiveness of an Interprofessional Patient Safety Team-Based Learning Simulation Experience on Healthcare Professional Trainees." *BMC Medical Education* 18, no. 1, 1–8. doi: 10.1186/s12909-018-1301-4

Henry, B.W., D.M. McCarthy, A.P. Nannicelli, N.P. Seivert, and J.A. Vozenilek. 2016. "Patients' Views of Teamwork in the Emergency Department Offer Insights About Team Performance." *Health Expectations* 19, no. 3, 702–715. doi: 10.1111/hex.12148

Jain, R. 2015. "Employee Innovative Behavior: A Conceptual Framework." *Indian Journal of Industrial Relations* 51, no. 1, 1–16. Retrieved from https://lopes.idm.oclc.org/login?url=http://search.ebscohost.com/login.aspx?direct=true&db=bth&AN=114168248&site=ehost-live&scope=site

Judge, T.A., and C.P. Zapata. 2015. "The Person--Situation Debate Revisited: Effect of Situation Strength and Trait Activation on the Validity of the Big Five

Personality Traits in Predicting Job Performance." *Academy of Management Journal* 58, no. 4, 1149–1179. doi: 10.5465/amj.2010.0837

Levine, S.R. 2011. "The Collaborative and Innovative Strategic Leader." *Credit Union Times* 22, no. 19, 12–18. Retrieved from https://lopes.idm.oclc.org/login?url=http://search.ebscohost.com/login.aspx?direct=true&db=bth&AN=60765042&site=ehost-live&scope=site

Maguirre, M.V., G.C. Ruelas, and C.G.D.L. Torre. 2016. "Women Empowerment through Social Innovation in Indigenous Social Enterprises." *RAM.Revista De Administracao Mackenzie* 17, no. 6, 164. doi: 10.1590/1678-69712016/administracao.v17n6p164-190

McKenna, P.J. 2017. "Strategies for Overcoming Obstacles to Change." *Of Counsel* 36, no. 7, 6–12. Retrieved from https://lopes.idm.oclc.org/login?url=http://search.ebscohost.com/login.aspx?direct=true&db=bth&AN=123824734&site=ehost-live&scope=site

Panaccio, A., D. Henderson, R. Liden, S. Wayne, and X. Cao. 2015. "Toward an Understanding of When and Why Servant Leadership Accounts for Employee Extra-Role Behaviors." *Journal of Business & Psychology* 30, no. 4, 657–675. doi: 10.1007/s10869-014-9388-z

Rehman, U., and M.G. Shahnawaz. 2018. "Machiavellianism, Job Autonomy, and Counterproductive Work Behaviour Among Indian Managers." *Revista De Psicologia Del Trabajo Y De Las Organizaciones* 34, no. 2, 83–88. doi: 10.5093/jwop2018a10

Schilling, J., and A. Kluge. 2009. "Barriers to Organizational Learning: An Integration of Theory and Research." *International Journal of Management Reviews* 11, no. 3, 337–360. doi: 10.1111/j.1468-2370.2008.00242.x

Steiner, G. 2009. "The Concept of Open Creativity: Collaborative Creative Problem Solving for Innovation Generation - A Systems Approach." *Journal of Business and Management,* 15, no. 1, 5–33. Retrieved from https://lopes.idm.oclc.org/login?url=https://search-proquest-com.lopes.idm.oclc.org/docview/211508893?accountid=7374

Stelmaszczyk, M. 2016. "Relationship Between Individual and Organizational Learning: Mediating Role of Team Learning." *Journal of Economics & Management* 26, no. 4, 107–127. doi: 10.22367/jem.2016.26.06

Tams, S., J.B. Thatcher, and V. Grover. 2018. "Concentration, Competence, Confidence, and Capture: An Experimental Study of Age, Interruption-Based Technostress, and Task Performance." *Journal of the Association for Information Systems* 19, no. 9, 857–908. doi: 10.17705/1jais.00511

Uhl-Bien, M., R. Marion, and McKelvey. 2007. *Complexity Leadership Theory: Shifting Leadership from the Industrial Age to the Knowledge era* doi: //doi-org.lopes.idm.oclc.org/10.1016/j.leaqua.2007.04.002

Valentine, M.A. 2018. "Renegotiating Spheres of Obligation The Role of Hierarchy in Organizational Learning." *Administrative Science Quarterly* 63, no. 3, 570–606. doi: 10.1177/0001839217718547

Van Iddekinge, C. H., and R.E. Ployhart. 2008. "Developments in the Criterion-Related Validation of Selection Procedures: A Critical Review and Recommendations for Practice." *Personnel Psychology* 61, no. 4, pp. 871–925.

Vaughn, K.R. 2016. "Leadership: Three Key Questions." *Tennessee Law Review* 83, no. 3, 803–812. Retrieved from https://lopes.idm.oclc.org/login?url=http:// search.ebscohost.com/login.aspx?direct=true&db=ofs&AN=117471310&sit e=eds-live&scope=site

Von Bertalanffy, L. 1968. *General System Theory,* 40. New York, NY.

Wallace, J.C., B.D. Edwards, J. Paul, M. Burke, M. Christian, and G. Eissa. 2016. "Change the Referent? A Meta-Analytic Investigation of Direct and Referent-Shift Consensus Models for Organizational Climate." *Journal of Management* 42, no. 4, pp. 838–861.

Wang, X., G. Wang, and W.C. Hou. 2016. "Effects of Emotional Labor and Adaptive Selling Behavior on Job Performance." *Social Behavior and Personality: An International Journal* 44, no. 5, 801. doi: 10.2224/sbp.2016.44.5.801

Weller, S.C., B. Vickers H.R. Bernard, A.M. Blackburn, S. Borgatti, C.C. Gravlee, and J.C. Johnson. 2018. "Open-Ended Interview Questions and Saturation." *Plos One* 13, no. 6 doi: 10.1371/journal.pone.0198606

Wemmer, F., E. Emrich, and J. Koenigstorfer. 2016. "The Impact of Coopetition-Based Open Innovation on Performance in Nonprofit Sports Clubs." *European Sport Management Quarterly* 16, no. 3, 341–363. Retrieved from https://lopes.idm.oclc.org/login?url=http://search.ebscohost.com/login.aspx?direct=true&db=s3h&AN=114819238&site=eds-live&scope=site

Woodley of Menie, M.A., D. Piffer, M.A. Peñaherrera, and H. Rindermann. 2016. *Evidence of Contemporary Polygenic Selection on the Big G of National Cognitive Ability: A Cross-Cultural Sociogenetic Analysis* 102, 90–97. doi: // doi-org.lopes.idm.oclc.org/10.1016/j.paid.2016.06.054

CHAPTER 3

The Role of Machine Learning on Future of Work in Smart Cities

Ammar Rayes

Abstract

Digitization, or the Fourth Industrial Revolution,[1] is driven by automation and information technology. It is causing massive market disruption in the job market regarding the future of work as machines are able to perform tasks better than human beings and are able to communicate with other machines to take the appropriate action. These machines are enabled by recent disrupted technologies including:

- *Cloud Computing and Virtualization*: Cloud computing allows companies to outsource their computing infrastructure fully or partially to public cloud and saves the cost of hosting all of their compute applications in a private data center. Recent data showed that the average network computing and storage infrastructure for a startup company in 2000 was $5 million.

---

[1] The First Industrial Revolution used water and steam power to mechanize production. The Second used electric power to create mass production. The Third used electronics and information technology to automate production. Now, a Fourth Industrial Revolution is building on the Third, the digital revolution that has been occurring since the middle of the last century. It is characterized by a fusion of technologies that is blurring the lines between the physical, digital, and biological spheres [5].

The cost in 2016 had dropped to $5000. This enormous 99% decline in cost was made possible by cloud computing [2].

- *Internet of Things (IoT)*: IoT is defined as the intersection of things (e.g., sensors), data, Internet, and standardized processes across multiple industry verticals. It allows machines to sense information at any time and communicate with other machines inexpensively and in real time.

- *Big Data*: Big data refers to extremely large structured and unstructured data sets that are difficult to analyze in real time with traditional data processing or computing systems. It is referred to as data with three "high Vs": high volume, high velocity, and high variety. Big data systems allow machines to analyze massive amounts of data and to produce intelligence in near real time. Companies are interested in big data applications to analyze extremely large data sets to reveal patterns, trends, and associations, especially relating to their customer behavior and buying patterns.

- *Advanced Wireless Networks*: Wireless networks are computer networks that use wireless data connections between network nodes. Wireless networks include licensed cellular network and unlicensed noncellular networks (e.g., WiFi, LoRa) allowing IoT and other devices to connect to the network and communicate.

At the top of the technology enablers are Artificial Intelligence (AI), Machine Learning (ML), and Deep Learning (DL). AI/ML/DL may be

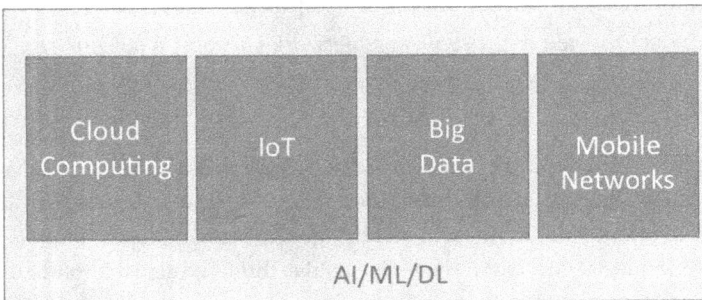

Figure 3.1 Relationship between AI/ML/DL and fourth industrial revolution technologies

considered as the brain of the overall system, as shown in Figure 3.1, with a job to make intelligent decisions.

Business leaders across the industry are convinced that AI/ML/DL can add significant value to their environment, bring efficiencies, lower their operating costs, and increase their market share. At the same time, the vast majority of such leaders are not sure where to start. One thing they're keen on is hiring experts with AI/ML/DL background.

This chapter first introduces AI, ML, and DL, and then provides use cases for the IT industry.

Artificial Intelligence, Machine, and Deep Learning

Artificial Intelligence (AI)

Artificial Intelligence (AI) is the overall concept of machines being able to perform useful tasks that a human being typically does, i.e., "intelligence of human being reproduced by machine."

AI was founded in the 1950s as an academic discipline and has experienced several waves of optimism since then. For instance, in the late 1960s, Marvin Minsky and Seymour Papert of the MIT AI Lab used AI in conjunction with various colors and blocks of various shapes and sizes to simplify the illustration of physics and sciences. They felt that physics and sciences were best understood by using simplified models like frictionless planes or perfectly rigid bodies [3]. In the early 1980s, Danny Hillis, a recent MIT graduate, enhanced AI by introducing the connection machine by utilizing parallel computing, a type of computation in which computation tasks are broken down into many smaller tasks and then carried out simultaneously [4]–[5]. The results are subsequently combined upon completion.

AI is used in object recognition, speech recognition, speech detection, natural language analysis, and painting creation, which are techniques for restoring or transforming parts of translations, missing parts from the whole.

Machine Learning (ML)

ML is a main application of AI and is based on the concept that "just give machines access to data and let them learn for themselves" for the purpose of predicting things correctly. ML can be defined as *the ability for a*

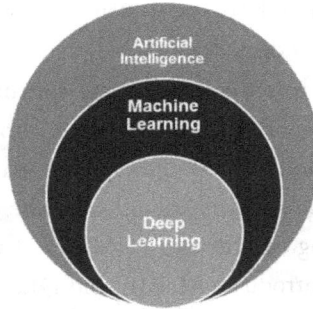

Figure 3.2 Relationship between AI, ML and DL

machine to learn from data with data, without being explicitly programmed to perform a specific task.

ML involves teaching a computer to recognize patterns by examples, rather than programming it with specific rules. Hence, ML creates algorithms or rules from data and make predictions on them.

Deep Learning (DL)

DL is part of a broader family of ML methods *based on learning data representations, as opposed to task-specific algorithms.* Learning can be supervised, semisupervised, or unsupervised as we'll show later in this chapter. Figure 3.2 illustrates the relationship between AI, ML, and DL.

It should be noted that the terms AI and ML are often used interchangeably especially by inexperienced users in generic industry.

ML Algorithm Categorization

This section breaks down ML algorithms into common categories and then lists the corresponding algorithms in each category. Specific examples will be provided in the next section. Given the large number of algorithms, we'll not be able to explain the details of each algorithm. We'll advise, therefore, that the reader reviews a basic technical ML book and/ or takes a training course online if needed.

In general, ML can be divided into three main categories: supervised learning, unsupervised learning, and reinforcement learning as shown in Figure 3.3.

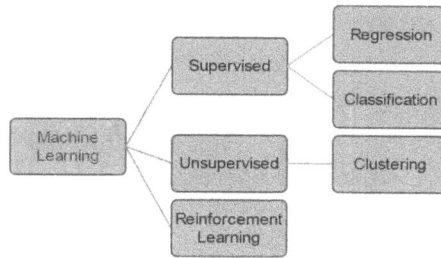

Figure 3.3 ML algorithm categorization

Supervised learning includes regression and classification techniques. Top examples of regression algorithms include: linear regression, support vector regression (SVR), Gaussian processes regression (GPR), ensemble methods, decision trees, and neural networks. Top examples of classification techniques include support vector machines, discriminant analysis, Naïve Bayes, nearest neighbor, and neural networks.

The main area of *unsupervised learning* is clustering. Top clustering techniques include: K-means, K-medoids, hierarchical, Gaussian mixture, Hidden Markov model, and neural networks. Both K-Means and K-medoids are partitioning clustering techniques that cluster the data set of n objects into k clusters with k known a priori. The K-medoids method is considered more robust to noise and outliers.

Reinforcement learning algorithms include Q-Learning, Sarsa[2] (an On-Policy algorithm for Temporal Difference Learning), and Deep Q-Networks [13]. The major difference between Sarsa and Q-Learning is that the maximum reward for the next state is not necessarily used for updating the Q-values.

Some readers may be asking by now what are neural networks and why do they appear in every ML category? Well, neural networks are systems patterned after the operation of neurons in the human brain. They "learn" with examples, generally without task-specific programming. For example, "neural networks might learn to identify images that contain people by analyzing example images that have been manually labeled

---

[2]   The name Sarsa comes from the fact that the updates are done using the quintuple Q (s, a, r, s', a'). Where: s and a are the original state and action, r is the reward observed in the following state and s', a' are the new state-action pair [12].

as "people" or "not people" and use the results to identify humans in other images. They do this analysis without any a priori knowledge about human, e.g., that they have two legs, two arms, a face with two eyes, two ears, a centered mouth, a nose, and human-like faces. Hence, neural networks evolve their own set of relevant characteristics from the learning material that they process [10].

Smart City Applications

Linear Regression

Linear regression is a simple approach for modeling the relationship between a scalar variable "y" and one or more explanatory variables "x". Hence, "x" is regarded as the descriptive independent variable and "y" is the outcome or dependent variable.

To establish a relationship / hypothesis, we place the independent variable on the x-axis and the dependent variable on y-axis and then try to find the best relationship between "x" and "y" variables with a straight line. As the independent variable "x" changes, the behavior of the dependent variable "y" is tracked with a sufficient number of observations[3] before the line is drawn.

Linear regression is often used in smart city applications to predict forecasting. For example, let's assume that we are trying to predict traffic congestion levels (e.g., 0–100% where 0 indicates nil congestion and 100% indicates a complete traffic jam) in a smart city as temperature changes. The first step is collecting data (x = temperature and y = traffic congestion level) over an adequate[4] period of time. Next, the collected data is divided randomly into two datasets: dataset 1 and dataset 2. Dataset 1 is used to plot the regression line (or hypothesis) and dataset 2 is used to verify that the regression line is placed correctly (or the hypothesis is correct), as shown in Figure 3.4. If the hypothesis is correct, then the regression line is assumed to be valid and may be used for future prediction. If not, then a new line should be drawn perhaps after collecting additional data.

---

[3] Methods to estimate the optimal number of observations are available in statistics but outside the scope of this chapter.

[4] As noted in the previous footnote, data collection period should be adequate to collect sufficient amount of data.

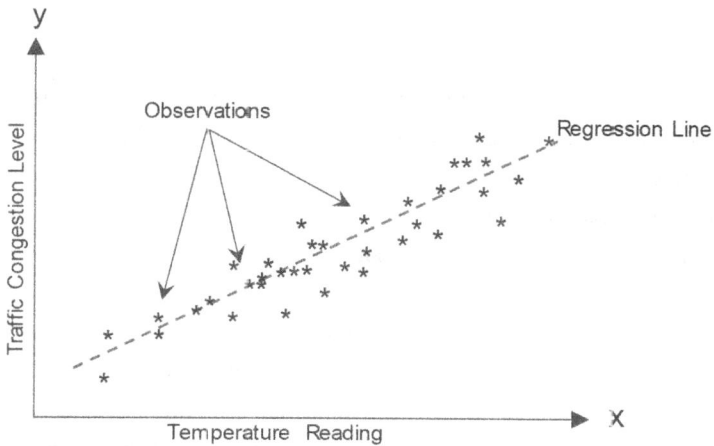

Figure 3.4 Liner regression example

It is important to note the following:

- Even if the model is correct for every point in dataset 2, there is no guarantee that the same model will always be correct for future data points. There are techniques in statistics to predict the predictability of certain events such as "entropy," which measures the amount of uncertainty or randomness in data. For example, the entropy for a fair coin is quite high (e.g., there is no way of determining what the outcome of the next toss even if the last 10 tosses show 3 heads and 7 tails) whereas the entropy of a coin with two heads is zero (the outcome is certain). This example illustrates the importance of collecting sufficient data.
- As stated earlier, the observed data should be always divided into two parts. One part (i.e., the large part, denoted as dataset 1 previously) should be used to construct the regression line (hypothesis) and the other part (dataset 2) should be used to validate the hypothesis (why this is important).

Decision Tree

Decision trees are also common machine learning techniques that are relatively simple to use and illustrate. They are used to explicitly represent decisions using branches (each branch represents a decision or an outcome) and leaves (each leaf node holds a class label). A decision node has two or more branches.

Cities around the world have been deploying sensors to measure temperature, wind speed, pollution, noise level, etc. IoT sensors are considered constrained devices (i.e., they have limited power and data processing capabilities) and often are placed in the open within a rough weather environment. Hence, sensors may fail and start reporting wrong information over a period of time.

In this example, we would like to build a model that predicts if an abnormal value is an indication of a problem (e.g., air pollution is too high) or if it is a "faulty reading" of the sensor. From history, we know that sensors fail due to their age, quality/brand (we'll track by the manufacturer and product identification (PID)), weather conditions (i.e., they may report wrong reading if the sensor is wet), wind conditions, and possibly other criteria.

Let's assume we collect the following data for a sufficient period of time (e.g., one year):

- Date and time
- Sensor's manufacturer: Vendor's name, PID
- Sensor's age in years
- Weather outlook: sunny, rainy, or overcast
- Wind conditions: strong or weak

Let's also assume that we take the "Sensor Data" as the first main attribute. The two subattributes of interest are then the sensor's PID (assuming that we have a list of faulty sensors based on PIDs) and the sensor's age (assuming that collected data showed that the sensor's quality degrades rapidly).

Now, assume that we observed a large number of faulty readings during high winds. Hence, we'll take the Wind Condition as the second main attribute. Finally, we'll take the Weather Outlook as the third and final attribute (Figure 3.5).

In general, attributes should be split further if the historical data did not provide confident answers with high probability. For example, we did not need to split the "Strong Wind" attribute further as the collected data consistently showed that sensors reported "faulty readings" during strong

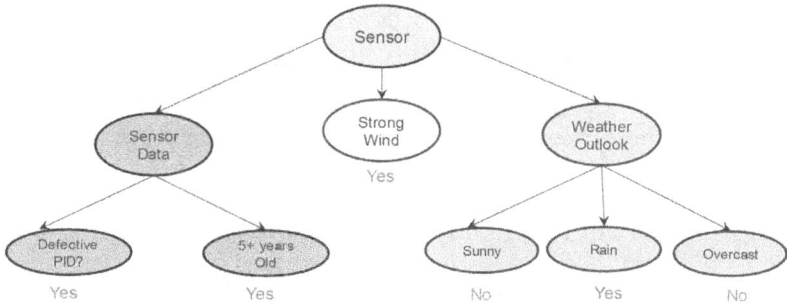

Figure 3.5 *Decision tree: Prediction model for defective sensors*

wind. On the other hand, if the historical data did not provide a confident answer, then additional subattributes should be added (e.g., "strong wind with rain" and "strong winds without rain" assuming the data is accurate when both "Strong Wind" and "Rain" conditions are tracked at the same time).

Based on the previous model, one can predict when a new sensor reading is wrong, that is, "Strong Wind" results in "fault reading" with very high probability (purely based on historical data).

Finally, in decision trees, it is a good idea to track the counts of positive and negative predictions at each node and use such data to build a confidence model. For example, assume that the data we collected so far consisted of 1000 measurements with 600 positives (i.e., correct faulty readings) and 400 negatives (incorrect fault readings) before any splitting. At this stage, 600/400 may be placed on the top of the "Sensor" node as shown in Figure 3.6 Now, let's assume that 323 readings in total were

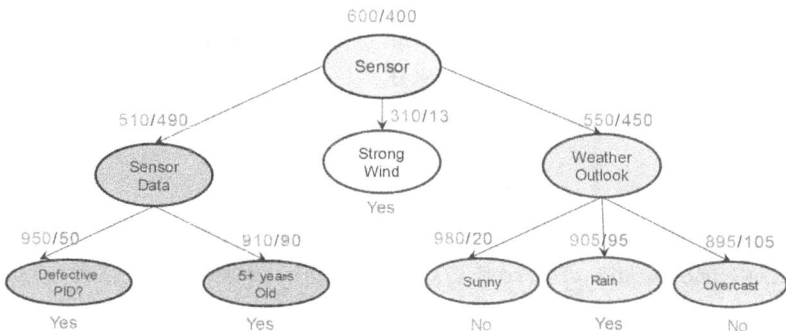

Figure 3.6 *Decision tree with confidence—Prediction model for defective sensors*

captured during "Strong Winds" with 310 positive and only 13 negative readings. Further data is illustrated in the figure. It should be noted that the confidence numbers should be updated as more data is collected. The addition of more data will of course result in better confidence.

6.3 K-Means Clustering Unsupervised Learning

K-means clustering aims to partition n observations into k clusters in which each observation belongs to the cluster with the nearest mean. This example focuses on optimizing energy usage in smart city data centers using K-mean clustering.

Smart city (or government) data centers generally consist of a large number of servers (physical machines (PMs)) that are grouped into multiple clusters. Each cluster manages and controls a large number of PMs. The centers offer computing services for various branches of government and agencies (called clients) and may charge them based on their usage. Clients submit requests to the data centers, specifying the amount of resources they need to perform certain tasks. Upon receiving a client request, the data center's cluster scheduler allocates the demanded resources to the client and assigns them to a PM. The virtualization technology allows the scheduler to assign multiple requests possibly coming from different clients to the same PM. Client requests are thus referred to as virtual machine (VM) requests.

With the "Green Initiative," energy optimization is very important to smart city's government and data center providers. It is important, therefore, to put servers to sleep when they are not in use. To do so, we have developed a novel technique to monitor PMs and effectively decide whether and when they need to be put in sleep mode. The solution framework has three major components: data clustering, workload prediction, and power management. A more detailed explanation of this solution is provided in the references [14]. In this example, however, we'll focus on how data clustering is utilized.

K-means clustering is used to create a set of clusters by group VM requests of similar characteristics (in terms of their requested resources) into the same cluster. Each VM request is mapped into one, and only one, cluster. The solution is evaluated using real Google traces [15] collected over a 29-day period from a Google cluster containing over 12,500 PMs.

The K-means algorithm [16] assigns n data points to k different clusters, where k is the a priori specified parameter. The algorithm starts by an initialization step where the centers of the k clusters are chosen randomly, and then assigns each data point to the cluster with the nearest center (according to some distance measure). Next, these cluster centers are recalculated based on the current assignment. The algorithm repeats by assigning points to the closest newly calculated clusters and then recalculates the new centers until the algorithm converges [15].

Figure 3.7 shows the resulting clusters for $k = 4$ based on the training set, where each category is marked by a different color/shape and the centers of these clusters c1, c2, c3, and c4 are marked by "x." Category 1 represents VM requests with a small amount of CPU and a small amount of memory; Category 2 represents VM requests with a medium amount of CPU and a small amount of memory; Category 3 represents VM requests with a large amount of memory (and any amount of requested CPU). Category 4 represents VM requests with a large amount of CPU (and any amount of requested memory.). Observe from the obtained clusters that requests with smaller amount of CPU and memory are denser than those with large amounts.

Conclusion

We'd like to conclude this chapter by restating the definition of AI, ML, and DL. AI is the overall concept of machines being able to perform useful tasks which a human being typically does, that is, "intelligence of

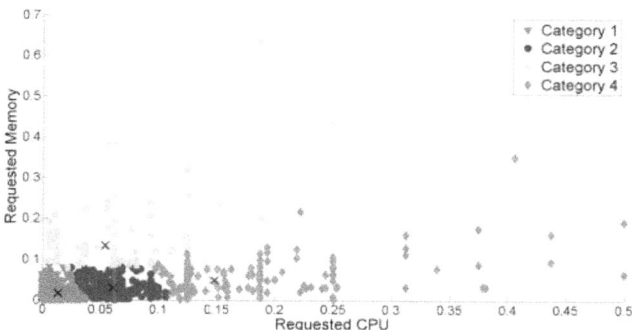

Figure 3.7 The resulting four categories for Google traces using K-means clustering [14]

human being reproduced by machine." ML is a main application of AI and can be defined as the ability for a machine to learn from data with data, without being explicitly programmed to perform a specific task. DL is part of a broader family of ML methods based on learning data representations, as opposed to task-specific algorithms. Learning can be supervised, semisupervised, or unsupervised.

This chapter introduced the main emerging technologies, namely cloud computing and virtualization, IoT, big data, and advanced wireless networks, coupled with AI/ML/DL. Next, the impact of the overall solutions on the future of work was shown. Three very specific smart city ML examples were provided in the areas of linear regression, decision tree, and K-means clustering unsupervised learning.

References

Schwab, K. 2016. "The Fourth Industrial Revolution: What it Means, How to Respond." *World Economic Forum Report*, January 14, https://weforum.org/agenda/2016/01/the-fourth-industrial-revolution-what-it-means-and-how-to-respond/

Rayes, A., and S. Salam. December, 2018. *IoT from Hype to Reality, the Road to Digitization*, 2nd ed., Springer.

Artificial Intelligence and Machine Intelligence, Wikipedia, https://en.wikipedia.org/wiki/Artificial_intelligence#Probabilistic_methods_for_uncertain_reasoningc

Morgan, July 2018. "Machine Learning Is Changing the Rules." O'Reilly Media, Inc, https://oreilly.com/library/view/machine-learning-is/9781492035367/

History of AI:_https://en.wikipedia.org/wiki/History_of_artificial_intelligence

Kanter, R.M. November 2011. "How Great Companies Think Differently." Harvard Business School, Issue: https://hbr.org/2011/11/how-great-companies-think-differently

Lemonlck, S. August 27, 2018. "Is Machine Learning Overhyped?" *Computational Chemistry* 96, no. 34, https://cen.acs.org/physical-chemistry/computational-chemistry/machine-learning-overhyped/96/i34

Chollet, F. December 22, 2017. *Deep Learning with Python*, 1st ed., Manning Publications, ISBN-13-078-16117294433

Harris, R. 2016. "More Data will be Created in 2017 than the Previous 5,000 Years of Humanity." *App Developer Magazine*, December 23, 2016. https://appdevelopermagazine.com/more-data-will-be-created-in-2017-than-the-previous-5,000-years-of-humanity-/

AI Neural Network, Wikipedia: https://en.wikipedia.org/wiki/Artificial_neural_network

Tiwari, S. Face Recognition with Python, in Under 25 Lines of Code, https://realpython.com/face-recognition-with-python/

Time Eden, Anthony Knittel and Raphale V. Uffelen, Reinforcement Learning Tutorial Online.

Quoc V. Le. 2015. "A Tutorial on Deep Learning, Part 2: Autoencoders, Convolutional Neural Networks and Recurrent Neural Networks." October 20, http://citeseerx.ist.psu.edu/viewdoc/download?doi=10.1.1.703.5244&rep=rep1&type=pdf

Dabbagh, M., B. Hamdaoui, M. Guizani, and A. Rayes. September 2015. "Energy-Efficient Resource Allocation and Provisioning Framework for Cloud Data Centers." *IEEE Transactions on Network and Service Management,*: http://web.engr.oregonstate.edu/~hamdaoui/papers/2015/mehiar-TNSM-15.pdf

Google Data Center Data Traces, November 2011. http://code.google.com/p/googleclusterdata/

Han, J., M. Kamber, and J. Pei. 2011. *Data Mining: Concepts and Techniques,* Morgan Kaufmann.

CHAPTER 4

Reskilling With AI

Pankaj Srivastava

Abstract

The fear that AI is going to displace many jobs is a popular theme in the media. Past waves of technological changes brought on by industrialization and computerization raised similar concerns. In each case, while there was some turmoil in the short term, there was net growth of employment in the long term as new jobs were created. What's especially true for this revolution is that AI is broad and powerful enough to address the very impact it is creating on jobs and careers of employees today. In this chapter, we discuss how machine learning and natural language processing can help address reskilling needs of organizations and support workers' needs. The approach relies on applying rigorous and comprehensive skill taxonomies, quantifying skill adjacency, prescribing optimal training actions and managing skill across the workforce. The approach can be a useful complement to talent management needs of organizations and the career development needs of workers.

Keywords

AI; reskilling; industrialization; jobs; career; professional skills; workers

Acknowledgments

I would like to acknowledge members of my team at IBM Chief Analytics Office that have contributed to developing the approaches described in this chapter especially Brian Johnston, Jonathan Debusk and Michael Peran.

Introduction: Business Imperative

The fear that AI is going to displace many jobs is a popular theme in the media. Almost on a daily basis, we come across news articles that suggest that automation and AI will displace many workers in the future. Ongoing technological advances such as self-driving cars, self-service stores without any cashiers, and so on, are stoking this fear. What is often not reported is that this type of displacement is hardly a new phenomenon. Past waves of technological changes brought on by industrialization and computerization raised similar concerns. History has shown us that each technological wave, while creating some disruption initially, has eventually paved the way for creating far more new jobs as well.

What's especially true for the AI revolution is that it can also be used in a positive way to serve the corporate and societal need for helping the workers that are impacted by it. By combining the evolving science of skill analytics and natural language understanding (NLU), we can create AI-based systems that can help workers whose skills are declining in demand and retrain them with the skills that are growing in demand in a most cost-efficient manner.

This chapter will cover approaches that are proving to be successful by applying rigorous and comprehensive skill taxonomies, measuring skill adjacency, prescribing optimal training actions, and managing skill across the workforce.

Skill Similarity

Any analytical approach has to start with a foundation in data. In this case, employees have to be categorized in terms of their skills in a structured taxonomy. While many employers have some type of classification for each type of corporate function, such as "sales" or "marketing," what is needed is a more comprehensive system that classifies each employee into a specific "skill." These skills can be aggregated into higher level categories such as "job roles." Since each employee can have multiple skills, it is possible to have primary, secondary, and even tertiary skills defined and stored in a comprehensive HR database. Also, each of these "job roles" and "skills" need to have a textual description that describes them.

When thousands of employees have been classified like this, it serves as a great foundation for developing a sophisticated approach to managing an inventory of skills and addressing demand/supply of skills. Since employees have multiple skills, the skill taxonomy can be used to designate "primary skill" and "secondary skill" for each employee.

When a particular skill that is needed to fill demand from clients, workforce managers have to determine whether employees with that skill are available. If they are not available, then the next best option is to see if employees with "similar" skills are available and can be quickly trained to perform the needed function. But how do we determine if a skill A is "similar" to a skill B?

At IBM, we developed an approach shown in Figure 4.1 where we combined three criteria to quantify the distance between skills so we can develop a method for measuring skill similarity.

- The first criterion considers the extent to which there is "co-occurrence" of pairs of skills as primary/secondary skills in the employee population. In other words, if skill A is often

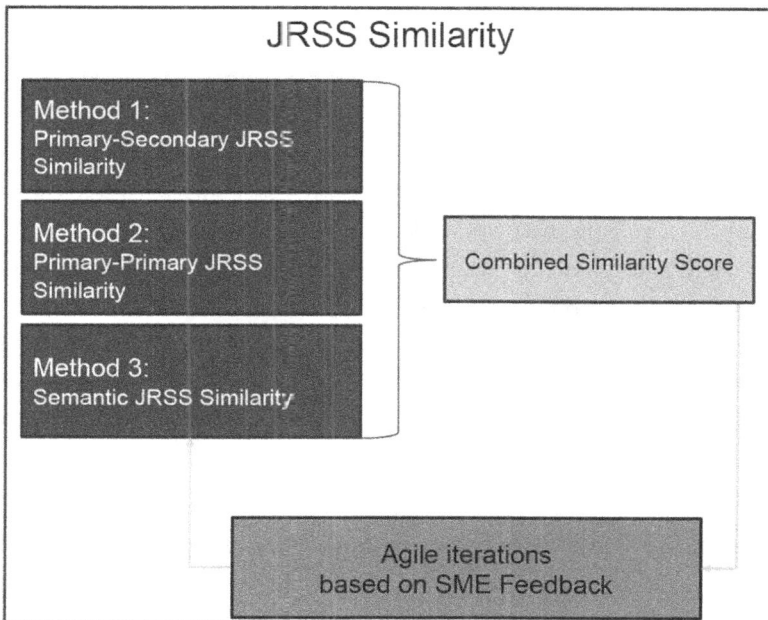

Figure 4.1 Job role—Skill set (JRSS) similarity approach

found to be present along with skill B (regardless of whether it is primary or secondary skill), then we can conclude that A and B are fairly similar.

- The second criterion considers the extent to which employees have transitioned from one skill to another over time. If many people have transitioned between a pair of skills, then we can conclude that they are likely to be more similar than a pair of skills that have never seen anyone transition from one to the other.

- The third criterion is based on the similarity of the textual descriptions of each pair of skills, which can be gleaned by applying NLP techniques. We established weights for each criterion and then tested the system by reviewing results with skill management experts to establish the validity of the skill similarity system. The system produced a "skill similarity index" value between 0 and 1 for any pair of skills.

Reskilling as a Service

Management executives are used to thinking of their business as a portfolio of products and services serving their clients. In a similar way, in the knowledge economy, management can also see their workforce as a portfolio of skills serving their clients. When they look ahead, as their business evolves, so will the need for various skills. A recent survey conducted by the World Economic Forum showed that on average 54 percent of employees will need to be reskilled to some extent over the 2018 to 2022 period (Figure 4.2).

Invariably, some skills may be in short supply within the company while other skills are in abundance. Filling the needs for skills in short supply through hiring is time consuming and expensive. It's much more effective to reskill existing employees and even subcontractors to meet demand. It's usually not practical to assume that every type of demand can be met through skilling but deciding exactly which ones can be met is challenging. It is especially difficult when the number of people to be reskilled is large and across a wide range of skills.

Reskilling needs
of less than 1 month, 13%

Reskilling needs
of 1–3 months, 12%

Reskilling
needs

No reskilling
needed, 46%

Reskilling needs
of 3–6 months, 10%

Reskilling needs
of 6–12 months, 9%

Reskilling needs
of over 1 year, 10%

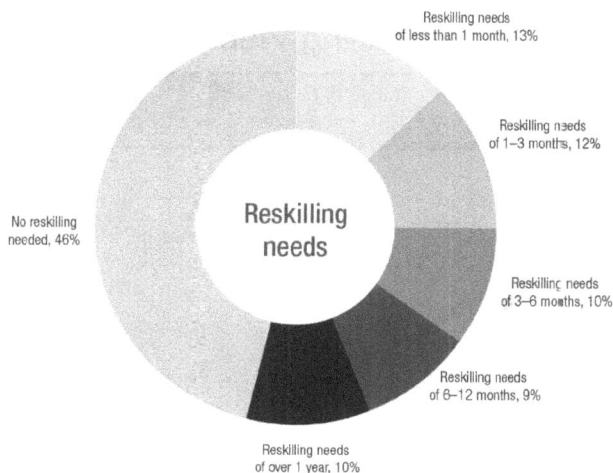

Figure 4.2 Expected average reskilling needs across companies, by share of employees, 2018–2022

Source: World Economic Forum report on Future of Jobs, 2018.

We have addressed this problem by combining skill similarity with training data to create training programs that address the needs to train workers for each skill. We take the employees that have skills in surplus and use Skill Similarity to determine which employees can be reskilled to perform the skills that are in high demand. While doing this, we take into account the training time that is needed to reskill the employee. HR learning programs provide the training time for a wide range of reskilling options. When the business starts implementing this on a continuous basis, the system starts learning from the success or failure of the reskilling process. The extent of reskill training time that is estimated early on gets refined as well. Figure 4.3 illustrates this idea showing groups of skill pairs where reskilling is viable as well as those where reskilling may not be viable because the training time required is too high.

This system needs to incorporate financial outcomes as well. By including estimated cost to hire or exit employees, the system can be trained to recommend the degree of skill similarity and the extent of retraining that should be accommodated to be financially beneficial. Figure 4.4 illustrates such a system. Client needs drive skill demand, which can evolve over time. Supply of skills is driven by hiring and ongoing training of

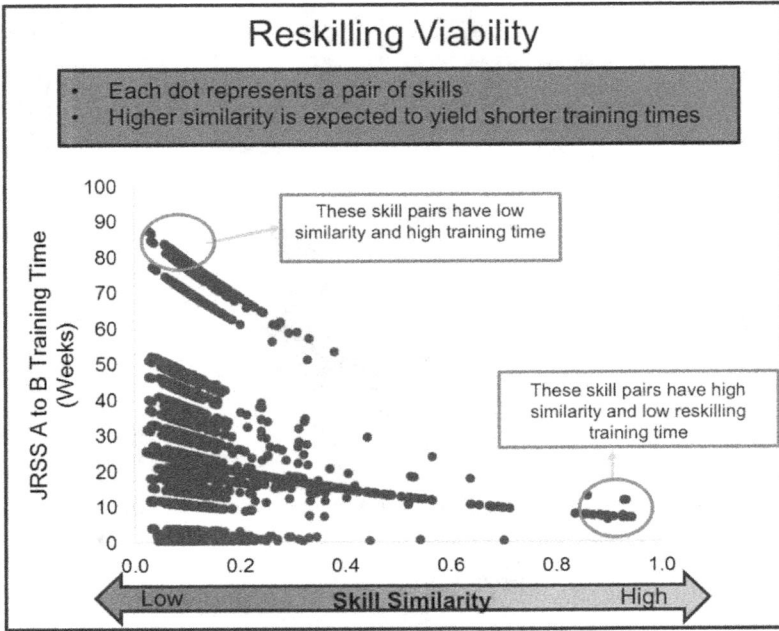

Reskilling Viability

- Each dot represents a pair of skills
- Higher similarity is expected to yield shorter training times

These skill pairs have low similarity and high training time

These skill pairs have high similarity and low reskilling training time

JRSS A to B Training Time (Weeks)

Skill Similarity

Low — High

Figure 4.3 Approach to determine reskilling viability

employees. Quantified demand and supply are used to establish skill gaps and gluts. The skill similarity approach described earlier in Figure 4.1 is combined with training time as shown in Figure 4.3 to determine which employees should be reskilled to meet demand. After these employees are trained and deployment, the system's success has be measured in terms of effectiveness of the employees who were reskilled. The extent of success can be used to further influence skill similarity, training time viability, and ultimately hiring and training of employees.

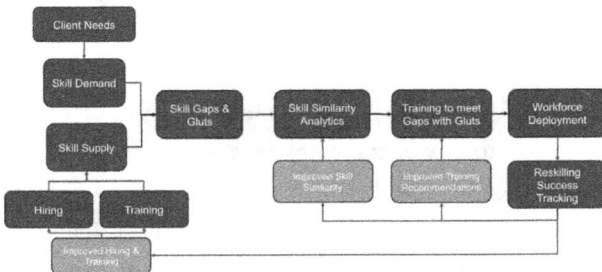

Figure 4.4 Workforce management system with reskilling

Conclusions

In this chapter, we discussed how machine learning and natural language processing can help address reskilling needs of organizations and support workers' needs. The approach relies on applying rigorous and comprehensive skill taxonomies, quantifying skill adjacency, prescribing optimal training actions and managing skill across the workforce. The approach can be employed to complement talent management of organizations and the career development needs of workers.

References

Autor, D.H. 2015. "Why Are There Still So Many Jobs? The History and Future of Workplace Automation." *Journal of Economic Perspectives* 29, no. 3, pp. 3–30.
Leopold, T.A., V.S. Ratcheva, and S. Zahidi. 2018. *The Future of Jobs Report*. The World Economic Forum.

CHAPTER 5

Is It Possible for Everyone to Be an Entrepreneur?

Jim Spohrer

Abstract

The popular press, as well as a growing number of academic publications, investigate the premise that artificial intelligence (AI) may destroy more jobs than it creates as AI capabilities grow. Others argue that AI is more like all previous technologies and will be a powerful tool to augment human capabilities—sometimes referred to as intelligence augmentation (IA). Consistent with the IA view, one proposed solution to the challenge of job automation/destruction is that more people may need to become entrepreneurs. The idea typically suggests that the use of low-cost digital workers (powered by AI) will help future entrepreneurs launch and scale their businesses via IA. But is it possible for everyone—or even most people—to be an entrepreneur? Probably not, but perhaps everyone can be part of an entrepreneurial ecosystem. This short chapter explores this question and the proposed solution from a service science perspective. As the cost of production drops, households will be able to meet more of their needs locally, leading to an increase in family-owned farms, factories, and professional service centers. As markets for personal data emerge, there will be benefits for individuals to incorporate.

Introduction: Motivations and Goals

In service research literature, there are a growing number of articles about the future impact of AI. The goal of this short chapter is to highlight a few items in service research literature, and then suggest future research directions. For example, Huang and Rust (2018) develop a theory of AI job replacement based on four intelligences (mechanical, analytical, intuitive, and empathetic), and suggest public policy to deal with this transformation is needed. Ostrom, Fotheringham and Bitner (2018) suggest barriers to the acceptance of AI in service encounters, noting especially the challenges of privacy concerns, trust, and perceptions of "creepiness." Both papers suggest that an extended adjustment period will be required as AI permeates an increasing range of roles and interactions in business and society.

Entrepreneurship and Individuals Incorporating

Ng (2018a) suggests that AI will cause a shift toward more entrepreneurship, specifically:

> *We propose that the rise of technology, strongly correlated with more gig workers and the rise of entrepreneurialism is not a coincidence, but a subtle trend where the global labour force attempts to "corporatize" itself that is, worker-becoming-a-firm that is owner managed, either through independent contracting or entrepreneurship, in the effort to increase opportunities for acquiring more resources, whether financial, human or social capital.*

Furthermore, in Ng (2018b) the ability to monetize personal data in an emerging AI-powered marketplace implies that everyone has something to sell and a route to market for digital goods. The benefits of selling assets as a corporation versus as an individual are also explored in these papers.

Rouse and Spohrer (2018) argue that the drop in the cost of digital workers will also lead to an increase in entrepreneurship and entrepreneurial activities. Spohrer (2016) argues that the fiduciary responsibility of business and governments to lower the cost of production will cause a transformation in which employees will become ecosystem partners, and hence will incorporate.

Service Science and Service Systems

The transformation of business and society brought on by increasing AI capabilities cannot be fully understood from any single disciplinary approach. Real-world problems rarely can be solved by applying the tools and techniques from just one discipline. However, disciplinary perspectives are important when they can be systematically integrated (Kline 1995). Service science is the study of service systems in business and society, and aims to provide a way to systematically integrate a wide range of disciplinary perspectives. More specifically, *service science is defined as an emerging transdiscipline that studies the evolving ecology of nested, networked service system entities, including their capabilities, constraints, rights, and responsibilities, especially their value co-creation and capability co-elevation interactions, as well as governance mechanisms* (Maglio and Spohrer 2008; Spohrer et al. 2013). *Service systems are defined as dynamic configurations of resources (people, technology, information, and organizations) interconnected internally and externally by value propositions to other service system entities* (Spohrer et al. 2007, 2008). Service system entities include individual people, businesses, universities, cities, states, nations, and other legal entities with capabilities, constraints, rights, and responsibilities (Spohrer and Maglio 2009). Service science is sometimes referred to as service science, management, engineering, design, arts, and public policy, to highlight the range of diverse disciplines it draws on, but does not replace the need for any of these (Spohrer et al. 2012, 2014). Legal entities (with rights and responsibilities) competing for collaborators exist in a constantly evolving ecology, and one in which AI systems are becoming actors (Spohrer et al. 2014, 2015, 2017, 2019). Service science is based on the world view known as the service dominant logic (Vargo and Lusch 2004, 2011, 2016). Service science also has a pedagogical component aimed at teaching "T-shaped" adaptive innovators (entrepreneurs) about the evolving ecology of service system entities (Donforio 2010; Spohrer 2016; Moghaddam et al. 2018).

Concluding Remarks

The challenge in this transformation is that there are a lot of smart ideas, but translating these ideas into a realistic life experience for society will be hard work. For example, Carter (2018) wrote:

> *There are a lot of smart people at MIT and around Boston working on technologies such as lidar that make driverless cars possible. I always*

say to these people, "Save a little bit of your innovative energy for the following challenge: How about the carless driver? What is to become of the tens of thousands of truck, taxi, and car drivers whose jobs are disrupted?" For these drivers, this unstoppable transition will be like the farm-to-factory transition. We owe it to them to make sure it all comes out well.

There is some hope, however, as evidenced in virtual and online game worlds. Bainbridge (2019, forthcoming) explores the online game world as a source of cultural change from the bottom up, and notes that:

Computer-controlled manufacturing technologies, combined with information technologies capable of supporting new forms of social organization, have the potential to take humanity far beyond the industrial revolution, to an economy in which many products of value in daily life are produced again locally in small workshops.

Now with modern technology we can miniaturize and more fully automate the family farm and factory, for example:

(1) Harvesting protein from the air: https://vttresearch.com/media/news/protein-produced-with-electricity-to-alleviate-world-hunger
(2) Creating an artificial leaf: https://technologyreview.com/s/601641/a-big-leap-for-an-artificial-leaf/
(3) Robotic recycling: https://www.recyclingproductnews.com/article/27382/ai-powered-robotic-waste-sorting-system-installed-at-zanker-recycling-facility http://service-science.info/archives/4525
(4) 3D-printed meat: https://cnet.com/news/3d-printed-meat-its-whats-for-dinner/
(5) Nearly limitless geothermal energy under every farm: http://thinkgeoenergy.com/could-a-new-approach-to-thermal-conductivity-revolutionise-geothermal/
(6) Starting a revolution in drilling technology: https://investors.com/politics/commentary/the-shale-revolution-is-a-made-in-america-success-story/

(7) Inventing better drilling technology for geothermal, etc: https://mercurynews.com/2017/11/22/elon-musks-earth-drilling-project-is-as-boring-as-ever/

(8) Revisiting Jefferson's idea for a highly productive local farm that provides for the household: http://ushistory.org/us/20b.asp

(9) Creating a secure and educated society through job training in the military: https://brookings.edu/experts/john-r-allen/

(10) And interconnect the youth of the world more rapidly: https://en.wikipedia.org/wiki/National_service http://www.un.org/millenniumgoals/

We need smarter/wiser service systems in the era of AI (Spohrer et al 2017) and the interconnected individual (Hasting and Saperstein 2018). This short chapter has just scratched the surface in exploring some service research literature related to the question, "is it possible for everyone to be an entrepreneur?"

References

Bainbridge, B. 2019. "Virtual Local Manufacturing Communities." In *Service Systems and Innovations in Business and Society Collection,* eds. A.T Lawrence and J. Weber. New York: Business Expert Press.

Carter, A. 2018. "Ideas America Needs to Align Technology With a Public Purpose: Disruptive Innovations Won't Produce a Better Society Unless We Work to Contain their Harms and Spread their Benefits." Ideas from Former U.S. Secretary of Defense. The Atlantic. Nov 25. URL: https://theatlantic.com/ideas/archive/2018/11/mark-zuckerberg-missed-opportunity/576088/

Donofrio, N., C. Sanchez, and J. Spohrer. 2010. "Collaborative Innovation and Service Systems." In *Holistic Engineering Education: Beyond Technology,* eds. D. Grasso and M. Brown Burkins, 243–69. New York: Springer.

Hastings, H., and J. Saperstein. 2018. "The Interconnected Individual: Seizing Opportunity in the Era of AI, Platforms, Apps, and Global Exchanges." In *Service Systems and Innovations in Business and Society Collection.* Business Expert Press.

Huang, M.H., and R.T. Rust. 2018. "Artificial Intelligence in Service." *Journal of Service Research* 21, no. 2, 155–172.

Kline, S.J. 1995. *Conceptual Foundations for Multidisciplinary Thinking.* Stanford: Stanford University Press.

Maglio, P.P., and J. Spohrer. 2008. "Fundamentals of Service Science." *Journal of the Academy of Marketing Science* 36, no. 1, pp. 18–20.

Moghaddam, Y., H. Demirkan, and J. Spohrer. 2018. "T-Shaped Professionals: Adaptive Innovators." In *Service Systems and Innovations in Business and Society Collection*. Business Expert Press.

Ng, I.C.L. 2018a. "Mimicking Firms: Future of Work and Theory of the Firm in a Digital Age." https://warwick.academia.edu/IreneNg

Ng, I.C.L. 2018b. "The Market for Person-Controlled Personal Data with the Hub-of-allThings (HAT)." Working Paper. Coventry: Warwick Manufacturing Group. WMG Service Systems Research Group Working Paper Series (01/18). http://wrap.warwick.ac.uk/101708/ doi: 10.13140/ RG.2.2.20917.78561

Ostrom, A.L., D. Fotheringham, and M.J. Bitner. 2018. "Chapter 5: Customer Acceptance of AI in Service Encounters: Understanding Antecedents and Consequences." In *Handbook of Service Science, Volume II, Service Science: Research and Innovations in the Service Economy*, eds. P.P. Maglio et al, 77– 104. New York, NY: Springer. Retrieved from https://doi.org/10.1007/978- 3-319-98512-1_5

Pakkala, D., and J.C. Spohrer. 2019. *Digital Service: Technological Agency in Service Systems*. 52nd HICSS. USA Hawaii Maui.

Rouse, W.B., and J.C. Spohrer. February 7, 2018. "Automating Versus Augmenting Intelligence." *Journal of Enterprise Transformation*, pp. 1–21.

Spohrer, J., P.P. Maglio, J. Bailey, and D. Gruhl. 2007. "Steps Toward a Science of Service Systems." *IEEE Computer* 40, no. 1, pp. 71–77.

Spohrer, J., S.L. Vargo, N. Casewell, and P.P. Maglio. 2008. "The Service System is the Basic Abstraction of Service Science", HICSS-41." In *Proceedings of 41st Hawaii International Conference on System Sciences*, 1–10. New York, USA: IEEE Press.

Spohrer, J., and P.P. Maglio. 2010. "Service Science: Toward a Smarter Planet." In *Introduction to Service Engineering*, eds. Karwowski and Salvendy, 3–10.

Spohrer, J., P. Piciocchi, and C. Bassano. 2012. "Three Frameworks for Service Research: Exploring Multilevel Governance in Nested, Networked Systems." *Service Science* 4, no. 2, pp. 147–160.

Spohrer, J., A. Giuiusa, H. Demirkan, and D. Ing. 2013. "Service Science: Reframing Progress With Universities." *Systems Research and Behavioral Science* 30, no. 5, pp. 561–569.

Spohrer, J., S.K. Kwan, and R.P. Fisk. 2014. "Marketing: A Service Science and Arts Perspective." In *Handbook of Service Marketing Research*, eds. R.T. Rust, M.H. Huang, and Edward Elgar, 489–526. New York NY.

Spohrer, J., H. Demirkan, and K. Lyons. 2015. "Social Value: A Service Science Perspective." In *Service Systems Science. Translational Systems Sciences*, ed. K. Kijima 2 vols. Tokyo: Springer.

Spohrer, J. 2016. "Services Science and Societal Convergence." In *Handbook of Science and Technology Convergence*, eds. W.S. Bainbridge and M.C. Roco, 323–335. Springer.

Spohrer, J. 2016. Innovation for jobs with cognitive assistants: A service science perspective, In Disrupting Unemployment (Ed. Nordfors D, Cerf V, Senges M), Ewing Marion Kauffman Foundation, Missouri, USA, (printed book) pp. 157–174.

Spohrer, J., M.A.K. Siddike, and Y. Kohda. 2017. "Rebuilding Evolution: A Service Science Perspective." HICSS 50, Proceedings of the 50th Hawaii International Conference on System Sciences.

Vargo, S.L., and R.F. Lusch. 2004. "Evolving to a New Dominant Logic for Marketing." *Journal of Marketing* 68, no. 1, pp. 1–7.

Vargo, S.L., and R.F. Lusch. 2011. "It's all B2B...and Beyond: Toward a Systems Perspective of the Market. *Industrial Marketing Management* 40, no. 2, pp. 181–187.

Vargo, S.L., and R.F. Lusch. 2016. "Institutions and Axioms: An Extension and Update of Service-Dominant Logic." *Journal of the Academy of Marketing Science* 44, no. 1, pp. 5–23.

PART II
Academic Perspective

CHAPTER 6

Thinking in 4T: Helping Workers Help Themselves With AI

Terri Griffith

Abstract

You see in 3D, and the future of work requires that all of us, not just organizational leaders, think (and act) in 4T. We all need fluency in how to integrate all of our talents, technology, and techniques as we work toward the targets of whatever our work is—whether paid work or the work of our lives. No silver bullets (Brooks 1987): relying on the dimension we're most comfortable with or have at hand.

This chapter is motivated by the growing application of artificial intelligence (AI) to work at all levels. For this chapter, I consider AI as a broad class of tools including hardware and software robots and intelligent devices. From basic rule-based automation to AI built on strategies of deep learning, we can apply new tools across much of our work. Possibilities range across colorizing movies, fraud detection, marketing lead generation, trip planning based on traffic conditions, foreign language translation, and depositing checks.

Top-Down and Bottom-Up

The application of AI and more basic automation is a top-down and bottom-up effort. Certainly, organizational management plays a massive role in providing direction and resources for next steps within the organization. The business press is rich with well-presented books on how to integrate automation into organizations. This is the most extensive and complete coverage I've ever seen on a topic I follow. A few of the excellent examples published this year:

- *Prediction Machines: The Simple Economics of Artificial Intelligence* (Agrawal, Gans and Goldfarb 2018)
- *Human + Machine: Reimagining Work in the Age of AI* (Daugherty and Wilson 2018)
- *Reinventing Jobs: A 4-Step Approach for Applying Automation to Work* (Jesuthasan and Boudreau 2018)

Each of these books offers a fairly top-down approach where the focus is on management action. Each does touch on, albeit briefly, what individual workers and teams should be doing to take advantage of resources and practices available today and how to prepare for the future. I extend from these AI/automation books in how individuals can, and should, work from the bottom-up.

The bottom-up approach to automation requires a different way of thinking and a different allocation of responsibility for job design than we typically see in the application of technology tools or management practices. Thinking in 4T requires evaluation and orchestrated application of talent, technology, and technique in service of specific targets. These ideas are aligned with academic studies of sociotechnical approaches to work (Trist and Bamforth 1951), and more recently, sociomaterial approaches (Cecez-Kecmanovic et al. 2014). Unfortunately, while broadly applicable, neither approach has received the kind of widespread attention and use that we see with more deterministic tools like Six Sigma approaches to process improvement or agile methods in software development.

Smart, well-resourced individuals and organizations predict vastly different overall effects on jobs as we see greater introductions of artificial intelligence and other forms of automation (Agrawal, Gans and Goldfarb 2019). The one thing experts agree on is that tasks within work will change and that this change will affect some workers more than others. Thinking in 4T is one way to prepare for these changes. It may be that individuals who Think in 4T as they adapt their work will be more protected from future job pressures than individuals who let the organization do the adapting from the top-down.

Why Contrast 3D and 4T?

Because 68 years of calling these ideas "sociotechnical systems theory" (Trist and Bamforth 1951) hasn't moved this critical idea into the mainstream. Work by Nobel Laureate Daniel Kahneman (2011) and others highlight how hard it can be to think with agency around complex issues. We need signposts to kickstart this thinking, and Thinking in 4T can be the first step. Marketing research suggests that simple tropes, like the juxtaposition of 3D and 4T, may serve as good reminders (Toncar and Munch 2003).

Connecting the Ts

Decades of research, starting with sociotechnical systems theory (Trist and Bamforth 1951) as noted earlier, have championed a systems approach to organization and work design (Parker, Morgeson and Johns 2017). Perhaps the most famous in technology settings is the imagery of Frederick Brooks, an A.M. Turing Award winner and team leader on the IBM System/360. Brooks writes, "...we see no silver bullet. There is no single development, in either technology or in management technique, that by itself promises even one order of magnitude improvement in productivity, in reliability, in simplicity" (1987, p. 10). We need to manage the 4Ts in concert.

Helping Workers Help Themselves With AI

Awareness of Artificial Intelligence

While Thinking in 4T was important in the past, it is now critical at all levels of organization and life. Institutional and individual interest in AI is on the rise. The National Science Foundation seems aligned with this perspective, citing "The Future of Work at the Human-Technology Frontier" (2018) as one of its 10 big ideas. Their focus: "Understanding how

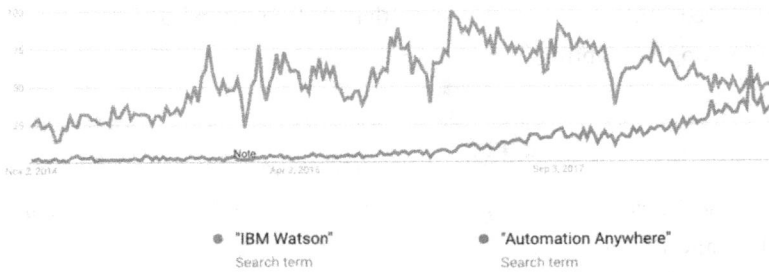

Google Trends Search. Numbers represent search interest relative to the highest point on the chart for the given region and time. A value of 100 is the peak popularity for the term. A value of 50 means that the term is half as popular.

https://trends.google.com/trends/explore?date=2014-11-01%202018-10-31&q=%22IBM%20Watson%22,%22Automation%20Anywhere%22

Figure 6.1 Worldwide relative search frequency for two branded automation platforms

constantly evolving technologies are actively shaping the lives of workers and how people, in turn, can shape those technologies, especially in the world of work."

Google searches for branded versions of automation are up dramatically since November 1, 2014 using the month Amazon Echo launched for the baseline (see Figure 6.1). However, even as we become more aware of the concept of AI, the AI technology lacks many of the triggers (e.g., Griffith 1999) that could help us think effectively about how to integrate it into our work. Even when we are aware that we are using AI, many of AI's functions can be a black box (Verghese, Shah and Harrington 2018).

Value of Thinking in 4T

Prior research suggests that the bottom-up approach to leveraging AI at work will be valuable to individual workers. Brenninkmeijer and Hekkert-Koning (2015) find that people who craft their work can increase their performance and employability. A worker who takes on the individual challenge of understanding his or her target, talent (knowledge, skills, and abilities), available technologies, and the techniques to bring these dimensions together within their role will be more likely to race with, rather than against, the "machines" (Brynjolfsson and McAfee 2011). That is, rather than go on the fool's errand of trying to best an AI or other automation on, for example, well-structured tasks that don't require dexterity, physical skill, or mobility, Brynjolfsson and Mitchell (2017) suggest using AI to augment tasks that leverage our human creativity and interpersonal skills.

It may also be that 4T-thinking workers find better roles as organizations transform within the Fourth Industrial Revolution (Schwab 2017). Thinking in 4T and taking action based on that thinking is critical for all of us. We all know our own work best. Thinking in 4T is a chance to take that work to the next level in a world of increasing change. Quoting Sophocles, "...heaven ne'er helps the men who will not act" (Plumptre 1978, p. 406).

That said, in organizational settings, work design that is both top-down and bottom-up (negotiated) has the most robust outcomes (Hornung et al. 2010). Let's help workers help themselves.

Triggering 4T Thinking

Applied psychology helps to explain why the application of integrated approaches like Thinking in 4T are difficult. Kahneman's (2011) best-selling general audience book, *Thinking, Fast and Slow*, highlights work on System 1 and System 2 modes of thinking, and this is an effective approach to understand the barriers and opportunities for augmenting work with automation. System 1 is automatic, quick, requires little or no effort, and presents no sense of voluntary control. System 2 thinking requires concentration, is complex, and has agency and choice. Kahneman offers an opening example (p. 19) of System 1 thinking in the form of a picture of an angry woman with tense eyes and an open mouth. He predicts, correctly in my case, that the reader's understanding of anger and likely next actions (e.g., speaking loud, unkind words) came instantly. His second example is the multiplication problem 17 × 24. Knowledge that is a multiplication problem came instantly (part of System 1), but the process to reach the answer would require steps of deciding whether or not to take on the task and then developing a process to do so (e.g., planning to hold the numbers in my head or getting a pencil and paper). This more procedural work is an example of System 2.

I see extant practices around change at work as being closer to System 1 than System 2. When we implement a change without clearly identifying our target, talent, technology, and technique we are more likely to go with what we know. We apply the status quo bias (Samuelson and Zeck-hauser 1988). In the most static form, we opt to continue with how we are already doing our work. In a slightly more dynamic version, the easier we can substitute AI for something we already do, the better rather than considering whether the overall approach should be adjusted.

Thinking in 4T requires a System 2 mindset. Thinking in 4T requires that we stop and consider our goals and available resources, consider trade-offs across the different resources, and then a practice to put them into play relevant to our work. System 2, Thinking in 4T in this case, is a challenge "if you are not ready or if your attention is directed inappropriately" (Kahneman 2011, p. 22).

Nudge Perspective

I'll offer six strategies for triggering Thinking in 4T. These build from another best-selling general audience book: *Nudge* by Nobel Laureate Richard Thaler and Cass Sunstein (2008). Thaler and Sunstein admit to taking some liberties with the initials, but they come up with a mnemonic (itself a nudge) to present their application of a variety of economic and psychological supports for changing behavior. Here I provide their nudge descriptor and then research supporting the approach as we consider Thinking in 4T and helping workers help themselves by augmenting their work with AI. The goal at the highest level is to create situations where using the 4T approach is easy and avoiding its use is more difficult.

Incentives

Intrinsic and extrinsic incentives are both predictors of performance, with intrinsic motivation playing a stronger role when there are less direct connections between performance and reward (Cerasoli, Nicklin and Ford 2014). Both intrinsic and extrinsic incentives can trigger the use of Thinking in 4T, or any other approach around the augmentation of work via AI or other automation. To the extent that workers see value outweighing the costs (or are helped to see), they are more inclined to act. Whether designing work for ourselves or for others, we need to highlight the connection between implementing AI in an integrative way and high-lighting the opportunity for rewards.

Understand mappings. Situations where experimenters ask partici-pants to do something, even something uncomfortable (e.g., get a tetanus shot), and then have participants specifically map how they will do it engender greater compliance than settings with general admonishments. (Leventhal, Singer and Jones 1965). I propose that Thinking in 4T to apply AI to an individual's work is much more enjoyable than a tetanus shot, but nonetheless we should apply similar techniques. Following from Gollwitzer (1999), helping workers create memorable if-then statements along the lines of, when thinking about how to take on a new task, I will take a stop-look-listen (Griffith 2012) moment, evaluate my 4T options, and then design an approach that takes each of the 4Ts into consider-ation. It may be that the best way to approach the target does not involve equal parts of talent, technology, or technique. It may be that the best application will use a subset of the Ts, though their interactions should be considered in order to find the best approach for the setting.

Defaults. The defaults nudge offers two distinct approaches: set the default such that AI/automation/augmentation of work is the default or acknowledge the status quo bias and put in place triggers for active think-ing. Louis and Sutton (1991) offer three approaches for switching from automatic (System 1) to active thinking (System 2): novelty (a situation that is perceived as new), discrepancy (a situation that is perceived as different from that expected), and deliberate requests for active thinking (a situation that may parallel the mapping request in the prior nudge). Griffith (1999) applied this perspective to evaluate triggers for sensem-aking around new technologies and notes that it is possible to design these triggers into the technology itself. AI or automation features that are specifically called out and highlighted as more core (versus tangential) and more concrete (versus abstract) will more likely trigger sensemaking around effective use, breaking people free from default approaches.

Give Feedback

It is hard to make good choices if we can't learn from choices made in the past (and ideally, also what would have happened had other choices been made). Task-provided feedback, where outcomes are directly observed during performance of the task, is the most immediate (Hall and Lawler 1968) and accurate source of feedback (Campbell et al. 1970). Task feedback is more informative than feedback originating from the supervisor (Greller and Herold 1975).

Expect error. In the physical world, this nudge is more of a preemptive guardrail. Thaler and Sunstein (2008) offer a variety of examples. Gas-specific connectors in medical environments such that misconnections are physically impossible. Google's backend automation within e-mail: When you attempt to send an e-mail that contains the word "attachment," but you have not attached anything, the system prompts you before allowing the send. Medication regimes being built to allow for more likely compliance—drugs that can be taken once a day in the morning, drugs packaged so that a pill is taken daily, even though the active medication is only 21 days a month. Designers understand that people fall back on habits when they can (i.e., not blocked by a connector that doesn't fit or an e-mail that doesn't send), or when context doesn't offer an incentive to avoid the error (e.g., Wood 2017, Louis and Sutton 1991). Cars with autonomous emergency braking offer a clear example of the value of this nudge. Use of this technology is documented to offer a 38 percent reduction in rear-end accidents (Fildes et al. 2015).

Structure Complex Choices

This last nudge is exactly what this chapter is about. For workers to integrate technology into their practice requires a complex negotiation across targets, talent, technology, and technique. To the extent that we can help people by offering a structure for their complex choices (focused on 4Ts, think of the mixing across the dimensions as a negotiation, Griffith 2012), we should.

Managing and Measuring Thinking in 4T

Once we trigger Thinking in 4T, we need to manage the approach like any other change. A focus on ability, motivation, and opportunity can drive toward performance (Blumberg and Pringle 1982). We can apply some Thinking in 4T ourselves. Our target is a shift in mindset from easier, System 1, silver bullet approaches to a goal-driven, multidimensional approach. The time seems right for this. Salas, Kozlowski, and Chen (2017), for example, offer the following in their 100-year review of applied psychology, "We need to start thinking in terms of human-system integration (e.g., Kozlowski et al. 2015) and think how selection, training, socialization, mentoring, leadership, and other domains will look like in the next century when technology is embedded in most organizational systems" (p. 595).

Talent comes in many forms. Earlier, I suggested some individual-level strategies for triggering Thinking in 4T. Much of our work is in teams and the growth of virtual teams in organizations is explosive (Dulebohn and Hoch 2017). While individual characteristics (knowledge, attitudes, traits, and abilities) are foundational to team practices and outcomes, teamwork, and innovation is an emergent, relational process (e.g., Burke et al. 2006). Grant (2009) notes:

> Relational perspectives focus on how jobs, roles, and tasks are more socially embedded than ever before, based on increases in interdependence and interactions with coworkers and service recipients. Proactive perspectives capture the growing importance of employees taking initiative to anticipate and create changes in how work is performed, based on increases in uncertainty and dynamism (p. 317)

We need to develop team-focused introductions to Thinking in 4T. Virtual teams, especially, use technology. Thinking in 4T for teams, and specifically, the application of AI, is powerful in such a setting.

Measurement is critical as we track across target, talent, technology, and technique. Goodman and Griffith (1991) offer a layered strategy that can be applied to measuring implementation success:

- Knowledge
- Attitudes
- Behavior/performance
- Normative consensus

The layered strategy acknowledges the dynamic nature of implementing any change. In the context of Thinking in 4T, the first layer is knowledge of the approach. Chapters/articles/blog posts, workshops, course sessions, and webinars are all part of the process I am using to share the ideas of Thinking in 4T. Measurement of knowledge is around knowledge of the four Ts, the ability to explain the use and value to others, and steps to using in individual, team, or organizational levels.

Attitudes come next as they, for better or worse, can precede interaction with the new tool or approach. Positive or negative feelings may ebb and flow as knowledge and experience buildup, and continued measurement can help with managing the process.

Behavior/performance can be mental or physical: Are people planning their application of AI to their work with a 4T approach? Is the identification of work targets part of the process and are resources considered across each of the talent, technology, and technique dimensions?

Normative consensus supports the focus on the relational aspects of the process. Once an application of AI is in place, is there a sharing process (Griffith 2012) that offers opportunities for reflection, improvement, and agreement that work should head in a particular direction. How widely held is the assessment? Does the approach diffuse beyond the initial application?

Concluding Remarks

My use of two best-selling books (*Nudge; Thinking, Fast and Slow*) is strategic. Thaler, Sunstein, and Kahneman are renowned scholars who found ways to describe evidence-based approaches to work and life that resonate with the broad audience we need to reach. Leveraging their effective language may offer deep support for the Thinking in 4T brand. Binding Thinking in 4T to the idea of seeing in 3D offers a trigger (Louis and Sutton 1991; Griffith 1999) to disrupt System 1 approaches to work and life with constantly changing technologies.

Responsibility for sharing new ways of thinking and working falls to all of us who understand that a silver bullet approach to how we engage with AI and other automation can't succeed. We should hold workshops on Thinking in 4T, design thinking, systems thinking, and so on. Lunch and Learns with vendors of light-weight AI (even if only around tools like Apple's Shortcuts app) may trigger colleagues to think about how they can individually craft their work. Face-to-face or virtual communities of practice (e.g., Griffith and Sawyer 2009) offer the chance to share success, get feedback, and develop norms around new ways of working.

And finally, we are in positions to continue to build evidence-based approaches to shifting new ways of working. Collaborations across professional networks, scholars, vendors of tools, and other organizations offer opportunities to share the ideas and the value of Thinking in 4T. Future research should first test these applications of psychology in work settings where AI offers clear value. Follow-on research could test different training tools, and evaluate how early in a person's experience the perspective provides value. We can assess technology designs in terms of their ability to trigger thinking in 4T (e.g., Griffith, 1991) or the value of default settings (e.g., Thaler and Sunstein 2009) that maintain System 2 modes.

References

Agrawal, A.K., J. Gans, and A. Goldfarb, eds. 2019. *The Economics of Artificial Intelligence: An Agenda*. Chicago, IL: University of Chicago Press.

Agrawal, A., J. Gans, and A. Goldfarb. 2018. *Prediction Machines: The Simple Economics of Artificial Intelligence*. Cambridge, MA: Harvard Business Press.

Blumberg, M., and C.D. Pringle. 1982. "The Missing Opportunity in Organizational Research Some Implications for a Theory of Work Performance." *Academy of Management Review* 7, no. 4, pp. 560–569.

Brenninkmeijer, V., and M. Hekkert-Koning. 2015. "To Craft or Not to Craft: The Relationships between Regulatory Focus, Job Crafting and Work Outcomes." *Career Development International* 20, no. 2, pp. 147–162.

Brooks, F. 1987. "No Silver Bullet—Essence and Accident in Software Engineering." *IEEE Computer* 20, no. 4, pp. 10–19.

Brynjolfsson, E., and A. McAfee. 2011. *Race against the Machine: How the Digital Revolution Is Accelerating Innovation, Driving Productivity, and Irreversibly Transforming Employment and the Economy*. Lexington, MA: Digital Frontier Press.

Brynjolfsson, E., and T. Mitchell. 2017. "What Can Machine Learning Do? Workforce Implications." *Science* 358, no. 6370, pp. 1530–1534.

Burke, C.S., K.C. Stagl, E. Salas, L. Pierce, and D. Kendall. 2006. "Understanding Team Adaptation: A Conceptual Analysis and Model." *Journal of Applied Psychology* 91, no. 6, pp. 1189–1207.

Campbell, J.P., E. Dunnette, E. Lawler, and K.E. Weick. 1970. *Managerial Behavior, Performance and Effectiveness*. New York: McGraw-Hill.

Cecez-Kecmanovic, D., R.D. Galliers, O. Henfridsson, S. Newell, and R. Vidgen. 2014. "The Sociomateriality of Information Systems: Current Status, Future Directions." *MIS Quarterly* 38, no. 3, pp. 809–830.

Cerasoli, C.P., J.M. Nicklin, and M.T. Ford. 2014. "Intrinsic Motivation and Extrinsic Incentives Jointly Predict Performance: A 40-Year Meta-Analysis." *Psychological Bulletin* 140, no. 4, pp. 980–1008.

Daugherty, P.R., and H.J. Wilson. 2018. *Human + Machine: Reimagining Work in the Age of AI*. Boston, MA: Harvard Business Press.

Dulebohn, J.H., and J.E. Hoch. 2017. "Virtual Teams in Organizations." *Human Resource Management Review* 27, no. 4, pp. 569–574.

Fildes, B., M. Keall, N. Bos, A. Lie, Y. Page, C. Pastor, L. Pennisi, M. Rizzi, P. Thomas, and C. Tingvall. 2015. "Effectiveness of Low Speed Autonomous Emergency Braking in Real-World Rear-End Crashes." *Accident Analysis & Prevention* 81, pp. 24–29.

Gollwitzer, P.M. 1999. "Implementation Intentions: Strong Effects of Simple Plans." *American Psychologist* 54, no. 7, pp. 493–503.

Goodman, P. S., and T. L. Griffith. 1991. "A Process Approach to the Implementation of New Technology." *Journal of Engineering and Technology Management* 8, nos. (3–4), pp. 261–285.

Google. 2018. "Smart Compose Comes to Pixel 3 and Four New Languages." Retrieved from https://blog.google/products/gmail/smart-compose-comes-pixel-3-and-four-new-languages/

Grant, A.M., and S.K. Parker. 2009. "Redesigning Work Design Theories: The Rise of Relational and Proactive Perspectives." *Academy of Management Annals* 3, no. 1, pp. 317–375.

Greller, M.M., and D.M. Herold. 1975. "Sources of Feedback: A Preliminary Investigation." *Organizational Behavior and Human Performance* 13, no. 2, pp. 244–256.

Griffith, T. L. 1999. "Technology Features as Triggers for Sensemaking." *Academy of Management Review* 24, no. 3, pp. 472–488.

Griffith, T.L. 2012. *The Plugged-in Manager: Get in Tune with Your People, Technology, and Organization to Thrive*. San Francisco: Jossey-Bass.

Griffith, T.L., and J.E. Sawyer. 2009. "Multilevel Knowledge and Team Performance in a Fortune 100 Technology Company." *Journal of Organizational Behavior* 31, no. 7, pp. 1003–1031.

Hall, D.T., and E.E. Lawler. 1968. "Unused Potential in Research and Development Organizations." *Research Management* 12, no. 5, pp. 339–354.

Hornung, S., D.M. Rousseau, J. Glaser, P. Angerer, and M. Weigl. 2010. "Beyond Top-Down and Bottom-up Work Redesign: Customizing Job Content through Idiosyncratic Deals." *Journal of Organizational Behavior* 31, nos. 2–3, pp. 187–215.

Jesuthasan, R., and J.W. Boudreau. 2018. *Reinventing Jobs: A 4-Step Approach for Applying Automation to Work*. Cambridge, MA: Harvard Business School Press.

Kahneman, D. 2011. *Thinking, Fast and Slow*: Farrar, Straus and Giroux New York.

Kozlowski, S.W.J., J.A. Grand, S.K. Baard, and M. Pearce. 2015. "Teams, Teamwork, and Team Effectiveness: Implications for Human Systems Integration." In *APA Handbook of Human Systems Integration*.

Leventhal, H., R. Singer, and S. Jones. 1965. "Effects of Fear and Specificity of Recommendation Upon Attitudes and Behavior." *Journal of Personality and Social Psychology* 2, no. 1, pp. 20–29.

Louis, M.R., and R.I. Sutton. 1991. "Switching Cognitive Gears: From Habits of Mind to Active Thinking." *Human Relations* 44, no. 1, pp. 55–76.

National Science Foundation. 2018. "NSF's 10 Big Ideas." https://nsf.gov/news/special_reports/big_ideas/human_tech.jsp (accessed May 11, 2018)

Parker, S.K., F.P. Morgeson and G. Johns. 2017. "One Hundred Years of Work Design Research: Looking Back and Looking Forward." *Journal of Applied Psychology* 102, no. 3, pp. 403–420.

Plumptre, E.H. 1978. *The Tragedies of Sophocles*. London: Daldy, Isbister & Co.

Salas, E., S.W.J. Kozlowski and G. Chen. 2017. "A Century of Progress in Industrial and Organizational Psychology: Discoveries and the Next Century." *Journal of Applied Psychology* 102, no. 3, pp. 589–598.

Samuelson, W., and R. Zeckhauser. 1988. "Status Quo Bias in Decision Making." *Journal of Risk and Uncertainty* 1, no. 1, pp. 7–59.

Schwab, K. 2017. *The Fourth Industrial Revolution*. New York: Crown Business.

Thaler, R., and C. Sunstein. 2008. *Nudge: Improving Decisions About Health, Wealth, and Happiness*. New Haven, CT: Yale University Press.

Toncar, M.F., and J.M Munch. 2003. "The Influence of Simple and Complex Tropes on Believability, Importance and Memory." *Journal of Marketing Theory and Practice* 11, no. 4, pp. 39–53.

Trist, E.L., and K.W. Bamforth. 1951. "Some Social and Psychological Consequences of the Long-Wall Method of Coal-Getting." *Human Relations* 4, no. 1, pp. 3–38.

Verghese, A., N.H. Shah, and R.A. Harrington. 2018. "What This Computer Needs Is a Physician: Humanism and Artificial Intelligence." *Journal of the American Medical Society* 319, no. 1, pp. 19–20.

Wood, W. 2017. "Habit in Personality and Social Psychology." *Personality and Social Psychology Review* 21, no. 4, pp. 389–403.

CHAPTER 7

Governance Challenges in the Age of Augmented Intelligence (AI): The Funny Business of Disruptions

P.K. Agarwal

Abstract

Beginning with the mainframe computers of the 1960s, we have witnessed wave after wave of tech-driven innovation. Interestingly each wave of technology becomes stronger than the previous one in its scope and reach causing disruption in its wake. Naturally, with each wave, some jobs are impacted but economic growth and new opportunities have so far compensated for these losses by the creation of new jobs. However, the newest wave propelled by Internet of Things, big data, machine learning, and artificial intelligence is exponentially stronger and has the potential of social and economic disruption at an unprecedented scale and speed.

There is a compelling need for public administrators to pay attention to these emerging forces and be prepared to smooth out the resulting social and economic impact for a large segment of society. The public administrators are likely to see a new set of challenges not witnessed before. There will be new demands that will strain the resources of government. There is an urgent need to rethink the role of government and lay the groundwork for serving the interests of the society.

Technological Disruption, Nothing New

By the 1870s, New Yorkers were taking over 100 million horsecar trips per year and by 1880 there were at least 150,000 horses in the city. Some of these provided transportation for people while others served to move freight from trains into and around the growing metropolis. At a rate of 22 pounds per horse per day, equine manure added up to millions of pounds each day and over 100,000 tons per year (not to mention around 10 million gallons of urine). Per one observer at the time, the streets were "literally carpeted with a warm, brown matting . . . smelling to heaven." So-called "crossing sweepers" would offer their services to pedestrians, clearing out paths for walking, but when it rained, the streets turned to muck. And when it was dry, wind whipped up the manure dust and choked the citizenry.

In the late 1800s, the "manure crisis" had become a problem in every major city in the world. *The Times* of London in 1894 did a linear extrapolation leading to a forecast that by the 1950s, London would be buried under nine feet of manure [1]. Without the benefit of history, one could easily romanticize the late 1800s as the pinnacle of clean technology. That was clearly not the case. This massive amount of horse excrement and carcasses were a major environmental and public health hazard.

A new disruptive technology was on the horizon. In 1870, Siegfried Marcus had built the first gasoline-powered combustion engine [2]. Karl Benz developed the first motorized vehicle in 1885 [3]. Henry Ford built his first experimental car in 1896 and formed the Ford Motor Company in 1903. By 1915, the Ford Motor Company was producing a million vehicles annually, and by 1927, it had produced over 15 million cars [4].

The disruption of the horse business was well on its way:

"Dispense with a horse and save the expense, care and anxiety of keeping it..."–An 1898 advertisement touting the benefits of owning a car (Figure 7.1).

Cars were replacing horses in the cities and tractors, as an alternative to horses, had started to appear on American farms. In 1917, Henry Ford introduced the Fordson, a wildly popular mass-produced tractor

Figure 7.1 Early automobiles

that ended up capturing 77 percent of the market in the following six years [5]. Tractors became the norm on American farms. The disruption of the horse was in full force on the American farm. Thus began a sharp, long-term decline in the number of horses used on American farms and cities, and a corresponding exponential increase in the number of tractors and cars.

The number of horses in the United States peaked at around 26 million in 1915 and steadily declined to around 3 million by 1960. Life became increasingly difficult for those in the horse business, whether in the cities or on the farms. This was true not only for those in the horse business but also for the ones lacking skills relevant for the emerging new economy. Farm unemployment was starting to emerge as a major social and political issue. The First World War temporarily alleviated the job crisis but jobs became even a more serious issue at the end of the First World War as soldiers came home. Such is the nature of disruption that accompanies innovation.

One hundred years later, we are in the midst of a social and economic transformation that is eerily similar to the one brought forth by the internal combustion engine. Except this time around the disruptions are being caused by computer technologies sweeping our landscape. During

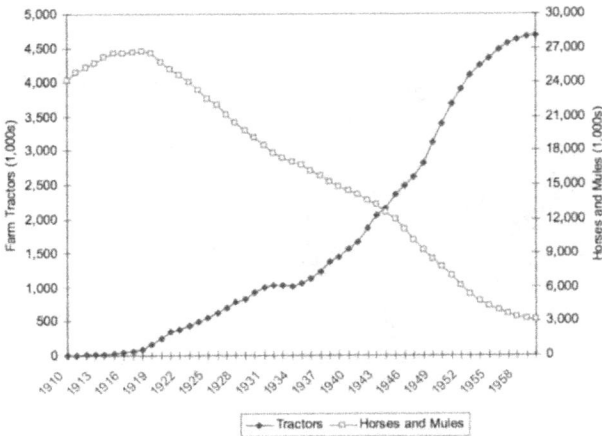

Figure 7.2 Early 20th century automation trends

the Industrial Revolution, we saw the horses and those in the horse business lose their jobs. In the current disruptive cycle, any job that is predictable and repetitive is at risk. Many call this the Fourth Industrial Revolution or Industry 4.0. Fast emerging technologies, such as Artificial Intelligence, Robotics, Machine Learning, Internet of Things, Blockchain, and Big Data propose to transform the economic and social landscape in the next couple of decades. These technologies will affect a very significant number of jobs in every country in the world. As if the Industrial Revolution was not disruptive enough, McKinsey Global Institute commented on the current situation: *"We estimate that this change is happening ten times faster and at 300 times the scale, or roughly 3,000 times the impact"* [6]. A forthcoming change of such intensity is going to create a very serious challenge for government. Moreover, it is currently not on the radar of most governments across the world. If governments do not begin to address this issue now, there is considerable risk of being late to the party and face the wrath of the large number of people impacted (Figure 7.2).

Disruption Comes in Waves Upon Waves

One of the key ideas in Steven Johnson's book, *Where Good Ideas Come From*, is that evolution and innovation usually happen in the realm of the adjacent possible, that is, innovation takes place adjacent to something else that is already in place. He gives the example of eBay, which could only happen until (a) someone had invented computers, which led to (b) a way to connect those computers, which led to (c) smaller computers, and then to the World Wide Web, and then eventually to eBay as a platform for online payments. Similarly, Uber could not have happened without mobile phones and the GPS. The notion of lone genius is a rarity. This "adjacent possible" creates a series of sequential waves and generally each wave tends to be stronger than the previous one in its scope and reach and its disruptive potential.

While electronic digital computers were around since the 1930s, the commercialization began with the mainframes in the 1960s. That led to wave after wave of innovation in the hardware front. The mainframe wave was followed by mini-computers, then PCs and networking, and then to the mobile devices. Similar innovation was taking place in the world of software. The convergence and maturity of hardware, software, and networking gave us the Internet. That led to the waves of application of the Internet. The first wave was the Internet of documents, followed by the Internet of commerce, the Internet of people (social media), and more recently the Internet of Things (IoT). Each wave builds upon the momentum created by the prior one and carries greater disruptive impact.

To clarify the increasing impact of each wave, Internet of documents gave us web pages and e-mail, initially connecting a few hundred million people. The next wave of e-commerce multiplied the user base by a factor of three to five. The next wave of social media or the Internet of People connected half the humanity. The newest wave of the Internet of Things will connect 20 to 30 billion things over the next four to five years [7]. The IoT will create a new world in which all things are connected and talking to each other and us.

These 20 to 30 billion connected things will generate massive amounts of data. Add to this to the data resulting from the innovations of other waves; we now face "infinite data" far beyond the ability of any human being to comprehend. This brings the tools of Big Data, Machine Learning, and AI to help make sense of this data. In the AI circles, there is considerable debate whether the rise of the machine is Intelligence

Augmentation (IA) or   AI. I believe it will be both. In some situations, machines will enhance and support human decisions and in other cases replace human in the performance of tasks. The AI or IA machines will need large quantities of data to learn the business. Accordingly, Clive Humby coined the phrase "*Data is the new oil,*" an apt metaphor for the relationship of data to learning machines.

Disruptions Redistribute Income and Create Income Disparities

It is hard to comprehend the extent of new wealth creation that happens alongside with disruptions. Imagine taking the valuation of FAANG (Facebook, Apple, Amazon, Netflix, and Google) companies and shop for established companies. The current combined valuation of FAANG companies is in excess of $3 trillion. Let us start with pricing the five most valuable automotive manufacturers: Toyota, Volkswagen, Daimler, BMW, and Honda. Their collective market cap is approximately $400 billion. The total market cap of five largest airlines— American, Delta, United, Emirates and Southwest—is about $31 billion. The five most valuable fast food brands—McDonalds, Starbucks, Subway, KFC, and Dominos—total to $210 billion. The world's largest retailer, Walmart, has a market cap of around $300 billion. The point of this is that the valuation of all of these well-known brands put together account for less than one-third of the valuation of the FAANG companies. I hope this provides a glimpse of the extent of new wealth creation. Why? Entrepreneurs upset the status quo and create new opportunities. These new disruptive companies show enormous potential for growth, both by from taking market shares away from existing players as well as creating new markets that did not exist before. Naturally, this new wealth tends to be concentrated among a few; entrepreneurs willing to take risks and those with skills that support the disruptive industries and ventures. In part, this would help explain the income gap and the shrinking middle-class phenomenon that we currently face. This has happened before. We saw the emergence of robber barons in the gilded age during the Industrial Revolution. To give an idea of the size and scale of this new wealth creation, the market cap of tech or tech-driven companies that have gone public in the last 35 years is in the $15 to $20 trillion range. By comparison, all of the gold in the world is valued at $8 trillion; the size of the U.S. economy is approximately $20 trillion [8]. At the individual level, of the top ten richest men in the United States (sometimes referred to as the three-comma club since a billion has three commas), seven have made their wealth in the tech or information sector. The collective net worth of these seven individuals is in excess of half a trillion dollars, equivalent to the entire economy of Sweden.

The Impact of Disruptions on Jobs

While the "horsepower" fueled the disruption during the Industrial Revolution, the current waves of disruption are fueled by computing technologies and its latest manifestations in the form of Machine Learning/AI and Robotics. These technologies are affecting the blue-collar as well as white-collar jobs. A recent report by the World Economic forum provides an interesting perspective on the job churn through 2022 [9].

> One set of estimates indicates that 75 million jobs may be displaced by a shift in the division of labor between humans and machines, while 133 million new roles may emerge that are more adapted to the new division of labor between humans, machines and algorithms. While these estimates and the assumptions behind them should be treated with caution, not least because they represent a subset of employment globally, they are useful in highlighting the types of adaptation strategies that must be put in place to facilitate the transition of the workforce to the new world.

As computers become more powerful and software more adept, we will see computers being able to mimic the five human senses. After all, it is our senses that define the humans to the rest of the world. With our computers interacting with us along the five senses, the distinction between humans and machines would begin to diminish. AI and Machine Learning will create human-like cognitive capabilities in computer hardware and software. The current applications of Machine Learning include natural language processing, handwriting recognition, computer vision, and other sensory perceptions. The keyboards will disappear as an artifact of the past. Keyboards were only necessary to provide very precise instructions to a slow, dumb computer. That is no longer the case and therefore a steady phase out of the keyboard. Further, what sets AI apart from prior technology waves is its ability to learn, then evolve, and take on more complex tasks and decisions. Thus, one can imagine that the more predictable and repeatable a job, the greater its potential of being taken over by machines.

A combination of Machine Learning and Robotics will replace low-end, labor-intensive jobs such as picking fruits and vegetables, cooking food, or car washing due to their predictability and repeatability. A recent startup in San Francisco, CafeX, now has a robot serving as a barista. There is early signs of the encroachment of machine learning (bots) into the jobs such as financial and sports reporting and financial advising. Machine Learning systems are showing great promise in interpreting images in the field of radiology and pathology.

Probably the most spectacular product of the Machine Learning and AI revolution is the autonomous vehicle. The potential for job disruption by the autonomous vehicle is huge. For starters, the transportation sector accounts for 7 percent of the U.S. economy. Approximately 5 million people are in the driving profession, which includes truck drivers, bus drivers, transportation for hire etc. A recent NPR report pointed out that truck, delivery, and tractor driving is the most common occupation in 29 of the 50 U.S. states [10]. The autonomous vehicles will also change the service model of personal transportation from ownership to transportation as a service, thus reducing the demand for passenger cars. This will affect jobs in areas such as vehicle sales, insurance, mechanics and engineers, parking lots, retail, and fuel. The health care sector will also feel the brunt of autonomous vehicles as the number of auto accidents would reduce dramatically (90 percent of all accidents are due to human error). The annual economic cost of road traffic accidents in the United States alone is around $242 billion (1.6 percent of our 2010 GDP). All this translates into jobs [11].

New Jobs Displace Old Ones

There are two distinct schools of thought of the future of jobs. The first group (pessimists) believes that we are destined for a jobless future in which machines will take over most of the jobs leading to a social crisis and anarchy unless public administrators act now. The other group (optimists) believe that disruptions create new wealth, new products and services, and new consumers. Economy will grow and standard of living will go up. However, both camps agree on one thing—many current jobs categories will disappear or shrink while new types of jobs will be created. Schumpeter's creative destruction in action! According to an Oxford study, 47 percent of all jobs are at some level of risk due to disruptions driven by cognitive capabilities of computers [12]. Therefore, no matter what, there is an upcoming massive need for reskilling people.

I am on the optimist side of this debate. Over the course of time, people become more productive due to disruptive technologies and economies grow. We create new products and services that could not have been even imagined a decade or two earlier. The more nimble of the existing companies transform themselves while new companies and industries emerge. Many countries, such a Singapore, reposition themselves to be successful in the new economy. Others go into a decline. Accordingly, we are starting to see the emergence of new job classes. Within the last ten years, we have witnessed the creation of new jobs that never existed before. Here are ten new job types that are growing very rapidly.

For instance, the number of app developers worldwide is estimated at eight to ten million. The number of registered drone pilots in the United

1.	App Developers
2.	Social Media Manager/Digital Marketing
3.	Cloud Computing Services
4.	UX Design
5.	Sustainability Expert
6.	Data Mining/Big Data Analysts
7.	Advanced Manufacturing Specialist
8.	Education/Admissions Consultants
9.	Genetic Counselor
10.	Drone Operator

States now exceeds 100,000 and growing. The U.S. Bureau of Labor Statistics forecast a 29 percent annual growth rate for genetic counselors between 2014 and 2024. Our greatest challenge in the next 10 to 20 years is not about having enough jobs, but finding the right fit between jobs and the people, especially those people whose jobs have been displaced by disruption and unable to reskill themselves for this new world order.

The Challenge for Governments

The AI-driven disruptive forces are also likely to cause significant change from the status quo for governments. Government will be forced into a significantly expanded role to manage the resulting crises.

Social Safety Nets

As AI and related technologies gain momentum, we are likely to see a large number of people whose jobs disappear and who would not be able to reskill themselves for the new type of jobs. Considering that robots would perform more of the routine manual work, public works programs such as the New Deal (or WPA) that provided relief during the great depression would have limited feasibility. To deal with the prospects of this potential mass unemployment coupled with aging demographics, many governments are experimenting with the concept of Universal Basic Income (UBI). A UBI is a type of program in which citizens would receive a regular sum of money from a source, typically government. UBI would have no means test and would be distributed to each person regardless of any changes to their financial status. There is no requirement to look for work and this would be independent of any other income. This is not a new idea and dates back to sixteenth century when Sir Thomas More argued this in Utopia. UBI is definitely gaining new ground in light of AI and has many proponents including notables, such as Elon Musk and Ray Kurzweil. Among the U.S. population, 48 percent of the people support this idea.

A more radical viewpoint on this issue of "survival wage" is to think of it as an income distribution problem. There is nothing wrong in principle if machines take over all of the mundane and repetitive work leading to abundance. The larger question is that who owns the means of production and for whose benefit. Speaking economics, in a scenario where machines do all the work, we could control the growth leading to an increased gross domestic product (GDP). In this scenario in which pie is larger and the population is more or less the same, could everyone not have a larger slice of the pie? In essence, if we could find a way to share this abundance, the entire society would be well off. In this scenario, it becomes a question of the collective political will of distributing income differently. Another less radical solution is to reduce the workweek from its current level in the United States of 40 hours a week. In the mid-1800s the average workweek was 70 hours. The workweek in the United States declined steadily since until the late 1950s when it averaged 40 hours. Since then it has remained at 40 hours per week. Henry Ford popularized the slogan of " 8 hours for work, 8 hours for rest, 8 hours for what we will" in the 1920s. Is there a modern day Ford who is willing to change the "8 hours for work" to "4 hours of work"?

"Show Me the Money"

One of the more serious consequences of AI-driven disruption would be a change in the revenue streams of government. If machines are doing a great deal of work traditionally done by humans, who pays the taxes. That has led many, including Bill Gates, to suggest that we ought to tax the robots [13]. The EU had also considered legislation that would tax the robots and use that revenue to pay for worker retraining. That legislation did not go through but most likely come up again as the issue of worker retraining becomes paramount. On a fun note, last year, the Saudi Government granted citizenship to a robot name Sophia, made by Hanson Robotics [14]. This was a first of its kind—a robot to receive citizenship of a country. One would imagine that if a robot can be a citizen, the privilege of paying taxes comes along with it. Incidentally, last November Sophia was named as the United Nations Development Program's Innovation Champion, the first nonhuman to be given a UN title.

Another example of how government revenues are likely to be impacted by the AI revolution is in the area of driverless cars.

A recent Deloitte Insights report states [15]: *"The US public sector will likely have to figure out how to offset anticipated declines in the $251 billion annually generated from fuel taxes, public-transportation fees, tolls, vehicle sales taxes, municipal parking, and registration and licensing fees. All these revenues are tied to today's reality of individually owned and operated vehicles—for instance, the need for parking diminishes with the rise of autonomous-drive shared mobility."*

It is hard to precisely quantify how much and how fast will the AI impact government revenues but some of the upcoming needs are obvious. The need for some sort of safety net, be it UBI or some other form, will rise soon. Investment in worker retraining on a large scale is a critical need. In addition, there is a critical need to upgrade the transportation, energy, and other urban infrastructures to support development of Smart Cities.

New Dimensions in Consumer Protection

Until recently, we had this utopian assumption that the AI machines will be free from human biases and therefore a progressive force for society. However, it is turning out that these machines are faithfully integrating the biases ingrained in the data used to train the machines.

John Giannandrea, Apple's Chief of Machine Learning and AI Strategy remarked, "It's important that we be transparent about the training data that we are using, and are looking for hidden biases in it, otherwise we are building biased systems. If someone is trying to sell you a black box system for medical decision support, and you don't know how it works or what data was used to train it, then I wouldn't trust it."

Similarly, Tom Simonite, writing for *Wired* magazine and describing research by Professor Vicente Ordóñez, said: "Their results are illuminating. Two prominent research-image collections—including one supported by Microsoft and Facebook—display a predictable gender bias in their depiction of activities such as cooking and sports. Images of shopping and washing are linked to women, for example, while coaching and shooting are tied to men. Machine learning software trained on the datasets didn't just mirror those biases, it amplified them. If a photo set generally associated women with cooking, software trained by studying those photos and their labels created an even stronger association."

It is easy to postulate that all historical data will have some biases along the lines of gender, ethnicity, or other demographics. We now run the risk of institutionalizing and possibly amplifying these biases. These machines might even find other correlations that are not that obvious to us humans.

Another source of AI related bias is through algorithms. Algorithms are rules, provided by human beings or machines that assist AI machines in making decisions. With increased sophistication, these algorithms are becoming more complex and in many cases, no one fully understands them. There have been suggestions that we will need to design new AI machines to decipher the reasoning behind the decision making of other AI machines.

A 2017 report from AI Now Institute recommends [16]:

Core *public agencies, such as those responsible for criminal justice, healthcare, welfare, and education (e.g., "high stakes" domains) should no longer use 'black box' AI and algorithmic systems. This includes the unreviewed or unvalidated use of pre-trained models, AI systems licensed from third party vendors, and algorithmic processes created in-house. The use of such systems by public agencies raises serious due process concerns, and at a minimum such systems should be available for public auditing, testing, and review, and subject to accountability standards.*

eGovernance and Services

The AI tools could be a real boon for government services. For a significant portion of the user of government services, including the elderly, the access to technology and the learning of how to use it is still a challenge. While most of the government services are now available online, the usage of government online service other than tax filings and motor vehicles is still somewhat limited. AI-enabled services could be a boon by bridging the accessibility and tech literacy gap. The greatest potential lies in the use of voice recognition systems. Thanks to exponential improvements in natural language processing (NLP), machine learning-based voice recognition systems last year achieved an accuracy of 95 percent, a tipping point, putting it on par with humans [17]. In some cases, there are claims of 99 percent accuracy in low-noise environments. Voice-based systems are ready for mass consumer usage. The rapid adoption of smart assistants/speakers enables the infrastructure needed for the delivery of these services. In effect, voice is what the webpage was in the 90's. It is the new browser.

While AI-enabled technologies offer significant opportunity, in general, governments are not well positioned to capitalize on these. They are barely playing catch up to the earlier generation of technologies. At present, more than half the traffic on the Internet is via mobile devices. Government are just getting around to migrating their services from the desktop to the mobile platforms. Now comes the challenge of voice enabling these eServices. Governments just do not possess these skillsets. There is an opportunity for the private sector to help bridge this gap. Done right, these could result in productive public–private partnerships. Done poorly, this could lead to de facto outsourcing of public services with government having little control over how these services get delivered.

On the innovation front, the EU believes that it should not matter where you live or how much you earn to have access to high speed Internet. To enable this, the EU is offering grants to localities to enable free Wi-Fi connectivity for citizens and visitors in public spaces such as parks, squares, public building, libraries, health centers, and museums everywhere in Europe through WiFi4EU.

Ensuring Individual Right to Be Left Alone

Louis Brandeis and Samuel Warren coauthored a landmark article for the *Harvard Law Review* in 1890 that defined protection of the private realm as the foundation of individual freedom in the modern age. This was in response to the new media of the time such as photography and other means of capturing and reproducing information. These new technologies gave increased capacity to government, press, and other entities too access previously unavailable details of personal activity. Brandeis and Warren argued for the law to evolve to deal with this technological change. Louis Brandeis subsequently as a member of the Supreme Court remained a champion of the "right to be let alone" as "the most comprehensive of rights, and the right most valued by civilized men."

Now, a century later, new technologies are forcing a very similar debate over the individual's right over their personal information and the right to privacy. The EU has taken a bold step with the General Data Protection Regulation (GDPR), which enables individuals to better control their personal data. This is still a work in progress and many assert that GDPR may be an overreaction to this growing problem. The Government of India is also considering similar measure to control the proliferation of personal information of its citizens and would prefer to keep it within the national boundaries.

It is the opinion of this author that data is now an asset as it has market value. Therefore, there is a critical need to establish who owns this data and what rights other related parties have over this data. At present, the de facto standard is that the various platforms own the data with limited control by the individual to whom the data pertains. For starters, one ought to have the right to opt out or better yet, to opt in for the capture of personal data. One could imagine a framework in which individuals own the data related to their personal, social, or commercial activity and they get to define the terms and conditions for the use of such data by other entities. This would make a significant impact in preserving privacy in the digital age.

Concluding Remarks

Governments are naturally slow to change because they have to be responsive to every single person in their constituency, including the proverbial "little old lady" who will go the DMV window to pay for her car registration in cash. Governments do not get to choose their customers. One cannot be like Amazon and choose the methods of delivery of services. On the other hand, technology offers new opportunities to reinvent government, and has the potential of making it more efficient and progressive. This gap is what keeps public administrators awake at night! When the pace of external change exceeds internal change, it can reach a tipping point and create a serious, sometimes irreversible, crisis for a government. With AI technologies, we are approaching that tipping point. There is an urgent need for public administrators to be proactive; they cannot simply wait. It is a rarity that even industry leaders are calling for the government to be more engaged, and more active in shaping policy and change. The time is now to seize the day!

References

Historic, U.K. 1894. "The Great Horse Manure Crisis of 1894." Retrieved from https://historic-uk.com/HistoryUK/HistoryofBritain/Great-Horse-Manure-Crisis-of-1894/

ASME. "Siegfried Marcus Car." Retrieved from https://asme.org/about-asme/who-we-are/engineering-history/landmarks/203-siegfried-marcus-car

ThoughtCo. "Biography of Karl Benz". Retrieved from https://thoughtco.com/karl-benz-and-automobile-4077066

Ford Website. "Company timeline". Retrieved from https://corporate.ford.com/history.html

Wikipedia. "Tractor." Retrieved from https://en.wikipedia.org/wiki/Tractor

McKinsey and Co. "The Four Global Forces Breaking All the Trends." Retrieved from https://mckinsey.com/business-functions/strategy-and-corporate-finance/our-insights/the-four-global-forces-breaking-all-the-trends

Statista. "Internet of Things (IoT) connected devices installed base worldwide from 2015 to 2025". Retrieved from https://statista.com/statistics/471264/iot-number-of-connected-devices-worldwide/

Wikipedia. "Gold Reserve" Retrieved from https://en.wikipedia.org/wiki/Gold_reserve

World Economic Forum. "The Future of Jobs Report 2018." Retrieved from https://weforum.org/reports/the-future-of-jobs-report-2018

NPR Planet Money. "Map: The Most Common Job in Every State". Retrieved from https://npr.org/sections/money/2015/02/05/382664837/map-the-most-common-job-in-every-state

U.S. Dept. of Transportation. "The Economic and Societal Impact of Motor Vehicle Crashes." Retrieved from https://crashstats.nhtsa.dot.gov/Api/Public/ViewPublication/812013

The Economist. "A Study Finds Nearly Half of Jobs are Vulnerable to Automation." Retrieved from https://economist.com/graphic-detail/2018/04/24/a-study-finds-nearly-half-of-jobs-are-vulnerable-to-automation

Quartz. "The robot that takes your job should pay taxes, says Bill Gates." Retrieved from https://qz.com/911968/bill-gates-the-robot-that-takes-your-job-should-pay-taxes/

Wikipedia. "Sophia (robot)". Retrieved from https://en.wikipedia.org/wiki/Sophia_(robot)

Deloitte Insights. "The Future of Mobility." Retrieved from https://www2.deloitte.com/insights/us/en/focus/future-of-mobility/transportation-technology.html

Medium. "The 10 Top Recommendations for the AI Field in 2017." Retrieved from https://medium.com/@AINowInstitute/the-10-top-recommendations-for-the-ai-field-in-2017-b3253624a7

Recode. "Google's ability to understand language is nearly equivalent to humans." Retrieved from https://recode.net/2017/5/31/15720118/google-understand-language-speech-equivalent-humans-code-conference-mary-meeker

CHAPTER 8

Policy Implications of AI

Stephen Kwan

Abstract

The U.S. economy is market-driven and the government plays a smaller role than in other countries where top-down policies and regulations are promulgated by the government. In this chapter we look at the recent views of the U.S. government and industry regarding policies for the future of jobs and artificial intelligence. Examples from other countries will be discussed to provide contrast.

Acknowledgment

P.K. Agarwal and Yosuke Takashima contributed to the breakout group discussion.

U.S. Position

The U.S. government had often taken the attitude of laissez faire by abstaining from interfering in the workings of the free market in driving its economy. In certain areas, the U.S. government had initiated and participated in "public, private partnerships" in working with industries to ensure U.S. competitiveness and foster leadership and growth in innovation. For example, the many programs at the National Institute for Standards and Technology (NIST) including cybersecurity, smart cities, advanced scientific projects, and technology partnerships with industries and academia.[1] In addition, the National Science Foundation (NSF) had

---

[1] https://nist.gov/tpo (accessed November 24, 2018).

also funded many basic research programs at universities and research institutions.[2]

Even though the U.S. government had funded and supported many research programs in advanced technologies, it had promulgated very few (if at all) policies and regulations regarding their development and application in industry. This is most evident in an event that was held at the White House, which resulted in the report "The National Artificial Intelligence Research and Development Strategic Plan" (OSTP 2016). In summary:

"This resulting AI R&D Strategic Plan defines a high-level framework that can be used to identify scientific and technological needs in AI, and to track the progress and maximize the impact of R&D investments to fill those needs. It also establishes priorities for Federally-funded R&D in AI looking beyond near-term AI capabilities toward long-term transformation impacts of AI on society and the world." (OSTP 2016, p. v).

This plan also laid out seven priorities: 1. Make long-term investments in AI research; 2. Develop effect methods for human–AI collaboration; 3. Understand and address the ethical, legal, and societal implications of AI; 4. Ensure the safety and security of AI systems; 5. Develop shared public datasets and environments for AI training and testing; 6. Measure and evaluate AI technologies through standards[3] and benchmarks; 7. Better understand the national AI R&D workforce needs (OSTP 2016, pp. 6–7).

The report indicated that even though there were some indications of impending increased shortage of AI experts reported by industry, there was no official data available. The report further recommended that additional studies were needed to better understand and address the current and future national workforce needs for AI R&D.

A more recent event at the White House discussed "..., the promise of AI and the policies we will need to realize that promise for the American people and maintain U.S. leadership in the age of artificial Intelligence" (OSTP 2018, p. 1) It also reassured the U.S. government's commitment

---

[2]   https://nsf.gov/funding/ (accessed November 24, 2018).

[3]   U.S. industry, academic, NIST and other U.S. government experts are active participants in the standards setting activities in the ISO/IEC JTC 1 Sub Committee on Artificial Intelligence which was formed in 2017.

to "… our free market approach to scientific discovery harness the combined strengths of government, industry, and academia, …" (OSTP 2018 p. 1 quoted Deputy Assistant to the President for Technology Policy Michael Kratsios). No specific policies were recommended but the key takeaways from the summit were: 1. Supporting the national AI R&D ecosystem; 2. Developing the American workforce to take full advantage of the benefits of AI; 3. Removing barriers to AI innovations in the United States; 4. Enabling high-impact, sector-specific applications of AI.

Of significance to the current discussion is the aforementioned item 2. The breakout session at the White House event included discussion about the need to prepare America for jobs of the future to match skill needs of industry with a renewed focus on STEM education, technical apprenticeships, reskilling, and lifelong learning programs. The discussion also recognized that "many existing occupations will significantly change or become obsolete" (OSTP 2018; p. 2). Recognizing that jobs will be lost in the future because of advances in AI and other automation technologies is an important step in building policies for the future. No detailed report or concrete action plan were made public after the event.

The notion that jobs will become obsolete and lost in the future because of advances in AI and other automation technologies is also recognized in industry and academia. Dr. Andrew Ng, a pioneer in AI, has been working on new educational structures on top of existing K1 to 12 and higher education that will help people succeed in the new economy. He also supported a conditional (e.g., study to gain new skills) basic income to combat job loss (Castellanos 2018). Some European trade unions and industry workers are proactively working with management so that they would reduce job loss and share the benefits of automation (O'Connor 2018).

The U.S. government has plans to support the AI industry and help develop the needed future workforce (OSTP 2018). To that end, there are executive branch activities such as designating AI as Administration R&D priority in the budget request to Congress (for an excellent summary, see Future of Life Institute 2018a). There are also some concrete legislative activities related to AI and the future workforce. Of note is H.R. 4829 "To promote a 21st century artificial intelligence workforce" (H.R. 4829 (2017–2018)). This bill is also known as the "AI JOBS Act of 2018." As of this writing the bill was referred to the Subcommittee on

Health, Employment, Labor, and Pensions. The U.S. government also recognized the potential of AI and other automation technologies to be applied to public service and its future workforce (e.g., see events by Partnership for Public Service (2018) and AAAI (2018)).

Even though there are activities in the executive and legislative branches of the U.S. government, some legislators, citizens, and industry groups are questioning the lack of a central policy focus on this important and growing industry where the United States currently has a leading role. They are starting to discuss whether the United States needs and should have a set of comprehensive AI policies (e.g., ITIF 2018, Delaney 2018, Carter 2018, Knight 2018).

On February 11, 2019, the White House announced that President Trump had signed an executive order "Maintaining American Leadership in Artificial Intelligence" (OSTP 2019, Presidential Executive Order 13859 (2019)). The Deputy Assistant to the President for Technology Policy Michael Kratsios also commented on the policy in an opinion piece (Kratsios 2019). This U.S. policy expressed the President's sentiment that "Continued American Leadership in Artificial Intelligence is of paramount importance to maintaining the economic and national security of the United States" (OSTP 2019). The policy is labeled as the "American AI Initiative" (*op. cit.*) that will be:

- Investing in AI research and development (R&D)
- Unleashing AI resources
- Setting AI governance standards
- Building the AI workforce
- International engagement and protecting our AI advantage

The Executive Order also calls on relevant U.S. government agencies to come up with proposals to implement the policy in the near future.

As the U.S. government and industries invest more and more in the innovation, development and deployment of AI technologies, other nations are also prioritizing AI for the benefits and betterment of their own industry and society (see section 2). As competition becomes more intense and politicized, trade and technology exchanges are increasingly coming under intensified scrutiny. The U.S. Department of Commerce is currently seeking public comments on potentially restricting export of "… certain emerging technologies [e.g., including AI and robotics] that are essential to the national security of the US" (Politi 2018).

Position of Other Nations

As mentioned in section 1, the U.S. government often has a light hand in setting industrial policies and regulations, instead it depends on public/ private sector partnerships in promoting and supporting industry prior- ities such as AI. Many other nations of the world have taken approaches ranging from one similar to the United States to where the practice is to promulgate top-down policies and regulations. An excellent survey of these policies can be found in (Future of Life 2018b). It listed interna- tional strategies for the EU, Nordic-Baltic Region, UN, UAE/India, G7, France/Canada as well as national strategies of Australia, Austria, Can- ada, China, Denmark, Estonia, Finland, France, Germany, India, Ireland, Italy, Japan, Kenya, Malaysia, Mexico, New Zealand, Russia, Singapore, Saudi Arabia, South Korea, Sweden, Tunisia, United Arab Emirates, the United States, and United Kingdom. These policies include formal national strategies, increase in budget to support AI research and edu- cation, legal framework for the AI industry, and a national white paper about AI. Other overviews of national AI strategies can be found in (Dut- ton 2018) and (Styslinger 2018).

In the following sections, examples from the U.K. and China are dis- cussed to compare and contrast the U.S. position.

Position of the United Kingdom

The UK government had developed a comprehensive and focused policy and action plan for the challenges of AI in industry and society. As a matter of fact, AI and Data are parts of four grand challenges that the UK govern- ment established as part of their industrial strategy (UK 2017). The Gov- ernment Office of AI and Center for Data Ethics and Innovation were also created to connect industry (e.g., the AI Council, an industry group) and the citizenry to the regulators so that their voices could be heard and heeded. Detailed responses from the UK government to the recommendations in the House of Lords AI Select Committee's Report provides a good review of the UK government's plan and missions (UK 2018).

The UK government agreed with the report that "… Blanket AI-specific regulation, at this stage, would be inappropriate. We believe that existing sector-specific regulators are best placed to consider the impact on their sectors of any subsequent regulation which may be needed" (ibid, p. 35). Furthermore, "… the Government committed to work with businesses to develop an agile approach to regulation that promotes innovation and the growth of new sectors, while protecting citizens and the environment" (op. cit.) The report also acknowledged that there will be a disruption in the labor market and jobs will be lost and created. The government's response reassured that actions will be taken to study, assess, and plan for education, re-education to prepare the workforce for the future. This is a good example of how a government partners with industry and heeds market forces to meet the challenges of emerging technologies for the benefit of society.

Position of China

In July 2017, the State Council of the People's Republic of China published the "New Generation Artificial Intelligence Development Plan" (PRC 2017). It was followed in December by the Ministry of Industry and Information Technology (MIIT) publishing the "Three-year action plan to promote the development of a new generation of artificial intelligence industry (2018–2020)" and its interpretation (MIIT 2017a,b). Dutton is accurate in saying that this policy is "… the most comprehensive of all national AI strategies, with initiatives and goals for R&D, industrialization, talent development, education and skills acquisition, standard setting and regulations, ethical norms and security" (Dutton 2018). The plan involved a great deal of top-down investment in both monetary and manpower terms. The plan also calls for Chinese companies endeavor to reach the same level as the United States by 2020, continue to make breakthroughs and become world's premier AI innovation center by 2030. The Chinese government intends to partner with national tech companies and industry groups such as the China Association for Artificial Intelligence (CAAI http://caai.cn/), the China Artificial Intelligence Industry

Innovation Alliance (CAIIA) to integrate resources and accelerate growth based on the plan (Future of Life Institute 2018c, Jing 2013).

This plan had engendered a lot of interest in the United States. Some have urged the U.S. government and industry to follow China's example (e.g., Knight 2017). Some have observed that the United States is already falling behind China because of the Chinese government and industry push (Lee 2018, Russel 2018). There are some signs that the Chinese impetus has been blunted by the current climate in trade and competition (Lucas 2018).

Concluding Remarks

In this chapter we have described the current status of U.S. position on AI and contrasted it with that of other nations with specific examples from the U.K. and China. Some common themes we observed are as follows:

1. National governments are starting to recognize that AI and emerging automation technologies will have profound effects on their industry, society, and citizenry. Many of these nations have started to establish strategies and plans (with various characteristics and degree of complexity) to meet the challenges head-on.

2. There is also recognition that the national workforce will be affected because of job loss and the gap in skills needed to meet the demand of new jobs. Some nations are starting to study the phenomenon and develop educational, retraining, and other actions to prepare their workforce for the future.

3. There are still a lot of unknowns as to the effect of AI and emerging automation technologies on industry, jobs, and society in general but we are seeing some concerted efforts in some nations to foster public/private partnerships, either top-down or market-driven, to meet the challenges.

References

All URLs were retrieved and verified on November 24, 2018 unless otherwise indicated.

AAAI. 2018. "Artificial Intelligence in Government and Public Sector". AAAI Fall Symposium Series. October 18–20. Arlington, VA. https://aaai.org/Symposia/Fall/fss18symposia.php#fs03

Carter, W.A. 2018. "A National Machine Intelligence Strategy for the United States." Center for Strategic & International Studies. March 1. https://csis.org/analysis/national-machine-intelligence-strategy-united-states

Castellanos, S. October 26, 2018. "AI Guru Andrew Ng on the Job Market of Tomorrow." *The Wall Street Journal.* https://wsj.com/articles/ai-guru-andrew-ng-on-the-job-market-of-tomorrow-1540562400

Delaney, J.K. (Congressman). 2018. "France, China, and the EU all have AI Strategy. Shouldn't the US?" *Wired.* May 20, 2018. https://wired.com/story/the-us-needs-an-ai-strategy/?mbid=social_twitter

Dutton, T. 2018. "An Overview of National AI Strategies." *Medium.com.* June 28. https://medium.com/politics-ai/an-overview-of-national-ai-strategies-2a70ec6edfd

The Future of Life Institute. 2018a. "AI Policy—United States." Future of Life Institute. https://futureoflife.org/ai-policy-united-states/

The Future of Life Institute. 2018b. "Global AI Policy. How Countries and Organizations Around the World are Approaching the Benefits and Risks of AI." https://futureoflife.org/ai-policy/

The Future of Life Institute. 2018c. "AI Policy—China." Future of Life Institute. https://futureoflife.org/ai-policy-china/

H.R. 4829. 2017–2018. "To Promote a 21st Century Artificial Intelligence Workforce." 115th U.S. Congress 2d Session. https://congress.gov/bill/115th-congress/house-bill/4829/text

ITIF. 2018. "Why it is Time for the United States to Develop a National AI Strategy." Information Technology & Innovation Foundation (ITIF) event scheduled for December 4, 1:00–2:30pm, 2018 at the Dirksen Senate Office Building, Room 562, 50 Constitution Ave NE, Washington, DC 20002. https://itif.org/events/2018/12/04/why-its-time-united-states-develop-national-ai-strategy

Jing S. 2018. "China forms 1st AI Alliance." *chinadaily.com.cn.* http://chinadaily.com.cn/business/2017-06/21/content_29833433.htm (accessed June 21, 2017)

Knight, W. 2017. "China's AI Awakening." *MIT Technology Review.* October 10 https://technologyreview.com/s/609038/chinas-ai-awakening/

Kratsios, M. 2019. "Why the US Needs a Strategy for AI." *Wired* Opinion, February 11, 2019. Retrieved 2/12/1091: https://wired.com/story/a-national-strategy-for-ai/

Lee, Kai-Fu. 2018. *AI Superpowers: China, Silicon Valley, and the New World Order.* Houghton Mifflin Harcourt, Boston New York.

Lucas, L. 2018. "China's Artificial Intelligence Ambitions Hit Hurdles." *Financial Times.* https://ft.com/content/8620933a-e0c5-11e8-a6e5-792428919cee (accessed November 14, 2018)

MIIT (2017a) "Three-Year Action Plan to Promote the Development of a New Generation of Artificial Intelligence Industry (2018–2020) [in Chinese]." Ministry of Industry and Information Technology (MIIT) of the People's Republic of China, 12/14/2017. http://miit.gov.cn/n1146295/n1652858/ n1652930/n3757016/c5960820/part/5960845.docx

MIIT. 2017b. "Three-year action plan to promote the development of a new generation of artificial intelligence industry (2018–2020) Interpretation [in Chinese]." Ministry of Industry and Information Technology (MIIT) of the People's Republic of China, http://miit.gov.cn/n1146295/n1652858/ n1653018/c5979643/content.html (accessed December 25, 2017).

O'Connor, S. 2018 "Trade Unions Seek Role in Age of Automation." *Financial Times,* https://ft.com/content/6d50b080-ad56-11e8-8253-48106866cd8a? segmentId=a7371401-027d-d8bf-8a7f-2a746e767d56 (accessed November 20)

OSTP (2016) The National Artificial Intelligence Research and Development Strategic Plan. National Science and Technology Council, Networking and Information Technology Research and Research Subcommittee. Office of Science and Technology Policy, The Office of the President of the United States. October. https://www.nitrd.gov/PUBS/national_ai_rd_strategic_plan.pdf

OSTP (2018) "The White House Hosts Summit on Artificial Intelligence for American Industry". Office of Science and Technology Policy, The Office of the President of the United States. May 10. https://whitehouse.gov/articles/ white-house-hosts-summit-artificial-intelligence-american-industry/

OSTP. February 11, 2019. "Accelerating America's Leadership in Artificial Intelligence." Office of Science and Technology Policy, The Office of the President of the United States." https://whitehouse.gov/articles/accelerating- americas-leadership-in-artificial-intelligence/ (accessed December 12, 2019)

Partnership for Public Service (2018) "Preparing the Future Work Force." Event held on October 23rd. Washington, DC. https://ourpublicservice. org/events/preparing-the-future-workforce/?utm_source=MASTER&utm_ campaign=8f5ed6ad04-EMAIL_CAMPAIGN_2018_10_09&utm_ medium=email&utm_term=0_3aed0f55fc-8f5ed6ad04-213567289

Politi, J. 2018. "US Considers export controls on AI and other new tech." *Financial Times,* https://ft.com/content/6ffc7756-ec58-11e8-89c8-d36339d835c0 (accessed November 19)

PRC. 2017. "New Generation Artificial Intelligence Development Plan [in Chinese]." State Council. People's Republic of China. July 20. http://gov.cn/ zhengce/content/2017-07/20/content_5211996.htm

Presidential Executive Order 13859. 2019. "Maintaining American Leadership in Artificial Intelligence". *Federal Register* 84, no. 31, Thursday, February 14, 2019. https://federalregister.gov/documents/2019/02/14/2019-02544/maintaining-american-leadership-in-artificial-intelligence (accessed February 15, 2019).

Russell, J. 2018. "China is Beating the US on AI, Says Noted Investor Kai-Fu Lee." *TechCrunch.* https://techcrunch.com/2018/09/05/china-is-beating-the-us-on-ai-says-noted-investor-kaifu-lee/?utm_source=tctwreshare&sr_share=twitter (accessed May 9, 2018).

Stik, C. 2018. "The European AI Landscape." *Report from Workshop, Brussels,* January 2018. European Commission. https://ec.europa.eu/digital-single-market/en/news/european-artificial-intelligence-landscape (accessed April 18).

Styslinger, I. 2018. "The Global State of Artificial Intelligence." *Disruptive Competition Project.* http://project-disco.org/innovation/050918the-global-state-of-artificial-intelligence/#.W_nlqnpKj1I (accessed May 9).

UK. 2017. "The UK's Industrial Strategy." UK Government Digital Services. https://gov.uk/government/topical-events/the-uks-industrial-strategy

UK. 2018. "Government response to House of Lords Artificial Intelligence Select Committee's Report on AI in the UK: Ready, Willing and Able?." Presented to the Parliament by the Secretary of State for Business, Energy and Industrial Strategy by Command of Her Majesty. June. https://parliament.uk/documents/lords-committees/Artificial-Intelligence/AI-Government-Response.pdf

CHAPTER 9

Conclusion

Across all industries, what makes the future of work different than what it was just a decade ago is the fast-changing technological advances especially in areas related to artificial intelligence (AI) fueled by machine learning (ML). This presents significant opportunities, but also many challenges at the societal, organizational, and individual levels. In this book, the chapter authors introduce a wide range of perspective on these challenges and opportunities:

Chapter 2: Tymann discusses that the future of jobs requires continuous learning for each individual on a team who must perform mainly two kind of roles: teacher and learner. These roles should rotate because each individual on a team is expert in a specific area and managers must create an adaptable culture of innovation and collaboration where employees are encouraged to work together and take risks.

Chapter 3: Rayes introduces AI and ML and their disruptive impacts on the future of jobs. He posits that the strength of AI and ML can be best realized by focusing on the overall service delivered to end customers, requiring full collaboration between diverse stakeholders across industry, academia, governments, and entrepreneurs. He sees three categories of jobs (1) jobs involving highly repetitive tasks with limited human interaction—for example, truck driver , (2) jobs involving nonrepetitive tasks with high human interaction—for example, surgeons using computer-guided lasers to remove tumors with greater precision, and (3) highly creative jobs that require design, judgment, leadership, entrepreneurship, or innovation. Rayes argues that the first category of jobs is highly susceptible to automation (and job loss), the second category lends itself to human–machine partnership (requiring reskilling), and the third category remains the realm of humans.

Chapter 4: Srivastava discusses how ML and natural language processing can help address reskilling needs of organizations and support workers' needs. The approach relies on applying rigorous and comprehensive skill taxonomies, quantifying skill adjacency, prescribing optimal training actions and managing skill across the workforce. The approach can be employed to complement talent management of organizations and the career development needs of workers.

Chapter 5: Spohrer explores some answers, through the service research lens, to the question, "is it possible for everyone to be an entrepreneur?" He argues that the main challenge in today's AI transformation lies in fact not in technological innovation but in translating all these smart technologies into a realistic life experience for society and people.

Chapter 6: Griffith argues that we need new ways of thinking and working, and she contends that there is no one-size-fits-all approach to how we engage with AI and automation. She proposes the 4T, talent, technology, technique in service, and target as framework that help us each chart our own water. She encourages collaboration across industry, academia, professional associations to continue to build evidence-based approaches to shifting new ways of working.

Chapter 7: Agarwal argues that governments are naturally slow to change because they have to respond to diverse set of constituents and they do not get to choose their customers. With the advent of advanced technologies including AI, the pace of external societal changes will be increasing far exceeding internal bureaucratic change. There is an urgent need for public administrators to be proactive in order to avoid serious social crisis.

Chapter 8: Kwan describes the current status of U.S. position on AI and contrasts it with that of other nations with specific examples from the UK and China. National governments are recognizing that AI and emerging automation technologies will have profound effects on their society, and to that end many have started to establish national strategies and plans to varying degrees to address job losses, displacements, and workforce retraining.

Appendix

Participants in the Discovery Summit, September 27, 2018

P.K. Agrawal, Northeastern University
Martin Fleming, IBM
Alex Kass, Accenture
Terri Griffith, Santa Clara University
Ann Majchrzak, University of Southern California
Ashwin Ram, Google
Preetha Ram, Harrisburg University of Science and Technology
Ammar Rayes, Cisco Systems (ISSIP President 2012–2013)
Jim Spohrer, IBM
Nathan Tymann, Cisco Systems
Jane Yin, Fujitsu
Heather Yurko, Facebook, ISSIP President
Yasunori Kimura, Japan Science and Technology Agency
Yosuke Takashima, Japan Science and Technology Agency
Yassi Moghaddam, International Society of Service Innovation Professionals
Rama Akkiraju, IBM (ISSIP President, 2018)
Steve Kwan, San Jose State University
Martha Russell, Stanford University
Mert Sezgen, EY
Brian Johnston, IBM
Pankaj Srivastava, IBM

About the Editors

Yassi Moghaddam is the Executive Director of International Society of Service Innovation Professionals (ISSIP), a nonprofit organization that promotes service innovation for our interconnected world. In this role, she has been catalyzing industry–academia collaboration to close the widening gap between education and employment leading to a thriving twenty-first century workforce, and to help institutions and individuals thrive in our digital economy. Yassi is also Managing Director of Stradanet, a boutique consulting firm that helps organizations create value through digital innovation and transformation. Her clients have included VMWare, Cisco Systems, Wells Fargo, EMC, Applied Materials, Northeastern University, and several startups. She holds an MBA from Columbia University, an MSc in Electrical Engineering (EE) from Georgia Tech, and a BSc in EE from University of Oklahoma. Yassi is coauthor of *T-Shaped Professionals: Adaptive Innovators* and a sought-after speaker.

Dr. Haluk Demirkan is a Milgard Endowed Professor of Service Innovation and Business Analytics, and Founder & Director of Center for Business Analytics and Master of Science in Business Analytics at the Milgard School of Business, University of Washington-Tacoma, and a Co-Founder & Board of Director of International Society of Service Innovation Professionals. He has a Ph.D. in information systems and operations management from the University of Florida. With 150+ publications, he has a global leadership in analytics and service innovation with cognitive computing and service-oriented technology. He has 20+ years experience advising 40+ Fortune 500 companies like IBM, GE, Cisco, HP, Intel, American Express. He has been a co-editor of a series "Service Systems and Innovations in Business and Society" at Business Expert Press since 2011.

Nathan Tymann is the Director of the People Strategic Advisory team at Blue Cross Blue Shield of North Carolina. His main areas of focus include enterprisewide strategic workforce planning and transforming the engagement model between human resources and partnering business units. In his career, he chose to challenge himself with complementary roles across a broad range of industries including food sweetener manufacturing, optoelectronics, telecommunications, and health insurance. He strives to model a growth mindset by seeking new opportunities to learn and to create. He earned a Bachelor of Arts degree in English Language and Literature from Gordon College, an MBA from Northeastern University, and is currently pursuing an EdD in Organizational Leadership in Organizational Development at Grand Canyon University. In his dissertation, he will study how leaders use collaboration to create innovation in organizations. Nathan enjoys consulting and speaking at conferences.

Dr. Ammar Rayes is a Distinguished Engineer / CTO at Cisco's Customer Experience Technology Office. He has authored over 100 publications in refereed journals and conferences on advances in software and networking related technologies, four books and over 35 U.S. and international patents. He is the Founding President and board member of the International Society of Service Innovation Professionals (www.issip.org), Adjunct Professor at San Jose State University, Editor-in-Chief of *Advances of Internet of Things Journal*, Editorial Board Member of *IEEE Blockchain Newsletter, Transactions on Industrial Networks and Intelligent Systems, Journal of Electronic Research and Application and the European Alliance for Innovation—Industrial Networks and Intelligent Systems*. He has served as Associate Editor of *ACM Transactions on Internet Technology* and *Wireless Communications and Mobile Computing* journals, guest editor of multiple journals and over half a dozen IEEE Communication or Network Magazine issues, cochaired the Frontiers in Service Conference and appeared as a keynote speaker at several IEEE and industry conferences: https://sites.google.com/view/ammarrayes/home. He received his BS and MS Degrees in EE from the University of Illinois at Urbana and his Ph.D. degree in EE from Washington University in St. Louis, Missouri, where he received the Outstanding Graduate Student Award in Telecommunications.

About the Authors

Pankaj Srivastava is a Vice President in IBM's Chief Analytics Office where he leads transformation initiatives that exploit Big Data, Advanced Analytics and AI. Mr. Srivastava has had extensive experience in technology development and business consulting across IBM's Cloud, Software and Services businesses and has worked across North America, Asia and Europe. Mr. Srivastava has driven revenue and profit growth through global strategic initiatives that have helped to transform IBM as well as many other companies in telecom and high-tech industries. His areas of expertise include applying cognitive and analytical techniques to Market Segmentation, Sales Coverage, Omni Channel Strategy, Sales Recommendation Systems and Workforce Transformation. He holds an MBA from The Wharton School, University of Pennsylvania, an M.S.E.E. from University of Connecticut and a B.Tech (Elec. Engg.) from IIT Bombay.

Dr. Jim Spohrer directs IBM's open source AI efforts in IBM's Open Technologies Group with a focus on open source developer and data science ecosystems. Previously at IBM, he led Global University Programs, cofounded Almaden Service Research, and was CTO Venture Capital Group. After his MIT BS in Physics, he developed speech recognition systems at Verbex, an Exxon company, before receiving his Yale PhD in Computer Science/Artificial Intelligence. In the 1990s, he attained Apple Computers' Distinguished Engineer Scientist and Technology title for next generation learning platforms. With over ninety publications and nine patents, he won the Gummesson Service Research award, Vargo and Lusch Service-Dominant Logic award, Daniel Berg Service Systems award, and a PICMET Fellow for advancing service science.

Dr. Terri L. Griffith holds the Keith Beedie Chair in Innovation and Entrepreneurship in Simon Fraser University's Beedie School of Business. Her research focuses on human and technical systems for the future of work, most recently the bottom-up application of automation. In 2012, she was honored as a Woman of Influence by the Silicon Valley Business Journal. Terri has served as a senior editor for Organization Science and associate editor for MIS Quarterly. Her undergraduate degree is from UC Berkeley; her MS and PhD are from Carnegie Mellon.

P.K. Agarwal, one of the most celebrated technology and academic leaders in Silicon Valley, serves as the Dean of UC Santa Cruz Extension in Silicon Valley. Prior to this, he served as Dean and CEO of Northeastern University—Silicon Valley, where he oversaw the development and growth of the university by creating innovative programs, working with major employers, and contributing to the economic vitality of the San Francisco Bay Area. Mr. Agarwal also serves as Chair of Future 500, a Bay Area-based pioneer in global sustainability. Formerly, he was CEO of TiE Global, an organization dedicated to fostering entrepreneurship across 61 cities in 18 countries. Prior to his tenure at TiE, Agarwal served as Governor Arnold Schwarzenegger's Chief Technology Officer for the state of California. Agarwal helped to pioneer the use of the Internet in government and has shaped national and state policy in this field, dating back to Al Gore's National Information Infrastructure Advisory Council in 1995. He also served as President of the National Association of State CIOs and the National Electronic Commerce Coordinating Council (ec3).

Dr. Stephen K. Kwan is Professor Emeritus in the Lucas College and Graduate School of Business at San José State University. He retired from being the Associate Dean of Graduate Business Programs and Lucas Professor of Service Science. He was the founding chair of the MIS department and had served as the Senior Associate Dean of the College. He is still actively involved in research and community activities in Service Science, Management, Engineering, and Design (SSMED), global e-commerce, service standards, and standardization. He was a recipient of multiple IBM Faculty Awards, grants from the National Science Foundation (NSF), and National Institute of Standards and Technology (NIST). He serves on the ISO/IEC JTC1 Sub-Committee 42 Artificial Intelligence, ANSI Committee on Education, ANSI Consumer Interest Forum, and the International Cooperation for Education about Standardization (ICES). He had published in the areas of Service Science, Queueing

Systems, Database Management, E-Commerce, Service Standards, Standards Education and Standards Policy. He received a B.S. and M.S. in Computer Science from the University of Oregon, and a Ph.D. in Management from UCLA.

How to Get Involved

We hope you found this book thought-provoking. If you would like to further advance your understanding of Future of Work and continue the conversation on this topic, we invite you to join our community at the International Society of Service Innovation Professionals (ISSIP), www.issip.org.

Index

OTHER TITLES IN THE COLLABORATIVE INTELLIGENCE COLLECTION

Jim Spohrer, IBM and Haluk Demirkan,
University of Washington, Tacoma, Editors

- *Everything Old is New Again* by Miriam Plavin-Masterman
- *Co-Design, Volume I* by Mark Gatenby and Stefan Cantore
- *Service Excellence in Organizations* by Fiona Urquhart
- *Obtaining Value from Big Data for Service Systems* by Stephen H. Kaisler

Announcing the Business Expert Press Digital Library

Concise e-books business students need for classroom and research

This book can also be purchased in an e-book collection by your library as

- a one-time purchase,
- that is owned forever,
- allows for simultaneous readers,
- has no restrictions on printing, and
- can be downloaded as PDFs from within the library community.

Our digital library collections are a great solution to beat the rising cost of textbooks. E-books can be loaded into their course management systems or onto students' e-book readers.
The **Business Expert Press** digital libraries are very affordable, with no obligation to buy in future years. For more information, please visit **www.businessexpertpress.com/librarians**. To set up a trial in the United States, please email **sales@businessexpertpress.com**.

www.ingramcontent.com/pod-product-compliance
Lightning Source LLC
Chambersburg PA
CBHW061335220326
41599CB00026B/5195